EVERYDAY
SURVIVAL KITS

EVERYDAY SURVIVAL KITS

EXACTLY WHAT YOU NEED FOR CONSTANT PREPAREDNESS

MARK PUHALY & JOEL STEVENS

IR

LIVING READY BOOKS
IOLA, WISCONSIN
www.LivingReadyOnline.com

CONTENTS

INTRODUCTION

Weather, power outages, a multi-faceted terrorist attack, and an outbreak of disease are a few examples of what can and has disrupted our normal daily lives in the last twenty years. Were you prepared then? Are you better prepared now? You need to be ready every time you step outside of your home or apartment. In this book we review every component of your life and help you think about where you can insert training or emergency kits that will help you survive almost anything. The keys to survival are situational awareness, knowledge, and the will to survive when other people would normally give up.

You need to be fit, tough, and mentally prepared if and when you find yourself in a survival situation. With mental preparedness comes thinking through situations and making sure you have the requisite gear at your disposal to help get you through a bad situation. You should not only think through these scenarios, but you should practice them. You should practice and train with the kit that is going to be with you so that you can evaluate what gear works best for you and be comfortable with it. Your kit should be easy to use, comfortable, and fit within your budget. Get your creative survival thoughts going and think about how you would come out on top in one of the survival scenarios described in subsequent chapters.

We have spent our lives thinking about different scenarios and testing survival gear for both the military and for personal use. We hope you find this book useful and put our information to practice. Whether you are just getting started or you are a veteran survivalist, use this book as a guide to make sure you have the necessary items to survive. From an elementary school student to a professional working in a high rise, this book has you covered with common-sense approaches for dealing with difficult situations.

The only person you can rely on in a survival situation is you. Ensure you have done your due diligence with regards to putting together your kit, studying the environment, and studying the potential threats that could cause harm to you and your family. The future belongs to those who are prepared. Make use of this book to make sure you are prepared and ready for anything.

CHAPTER ONE

PURSE SURVIVAL KIT

THE SURVIVAL SCENARIO

Just after Valentine's Day 2011, a 33-year-old woman was assaulted and robbed outside the downtown post office in a small Oregon college town before 7 a.m. She was grabbed from behind as she was getting into her vehicle and struck on the head several times with a blunt object before being knocked to the ground. The attacker then proceeded to steal her purse and other personal items.

The woman took several minutes before she was able to call 9-1-1. She was transported to a local hospital for treatment of non-life-threatening injuries. Her purse was later located in bushes close to the post office. Several other items were not recovered by the police. The unidentified male attacker was described as a middle-aged man with a pockmarked face and rotten teeth. He was last seen running north through the streets and he remained at large the evening of the attack.

THE ANALYSIS

How many of us have gone to the post office in the early morning hours prior to going to work? A scenario like this could happen to anyone, especially if you're not prepared or expecting

PURSE SURVIVAL KIT GEAR LIST

- ☐ Purse
- ☐ Phone
- ☐ Phone charger (wall adapter)
- ☐ Mirror
- ☐ Lighter
- ☐ Bright-colored scarf
- ☐ Whistle
- ☐ Mace/pepper spray or a Taser
- ☐ Pistol (if you have a concealed weapons permit where you live)
- ☐ Kubaton or tactical baton
- ☐ Umbrella or walking stick
- ☐ Knife (Swiss Army or survival knife)
- ☐ Wrist compass or mini compass
- ☐ Water bottle
- ☐ Food (snacks or energy bars)
- ☐ Basic first aid kit (small and compact)
- ☐ Emergency blanket (space blanket)
- ☐ Cash ($20 to $100)

danger in the most unlikely of places. This woman did not expect to get bashed in the head while pulling the keys out of her purse. She was probably doing what she has done hundreds of times before and expected nothing out of the ordinary to happen to her.

What could she have done differently? Could she have gone later in the day? Was it still dark out that morning? Was she alone in the parking lot? What else did she have in her purse? Did she have anything to ward off an attacker? What could she have had in her purse that she could carry every day that could have possibly prevented this from happening? These are the questions you should consider when you are by yourself in public places, both familiar and unfamiliar.

When it comes to being prepared, your environment doesn't matter. Emergencies can happen anywhere—in a rural or urban area, in a relatively safe, gated community, and in shopping centers. There have been reports of people being abducted in every type of environment–rich, poor, in daylight, after dark, at dusk, and at dawn. You have to be prepared, even in what you perceive to be the most secure of environments. Those who fail to prepare will not have a fighting chance to survive an emergency.

THE TAKEAWAY

Purses are usually used to carry a wallet, phone, personal care items, and makeup. It might also include a tablet or laptop and phone charger. Obviously, the larger the purse, the more you can fit in it. I've often commented on women's purses that could be used as weapons because they are so heavy and could easily be swung against an attacker. Why not add a few items to your purse that could potentially save your life and get you out alive if faced with a survival situation?

Purse

Phone and Charger

PURSE SURVIVAL KIT

The items in the purse survival kit are in addition to the normal day-to-day items you already carry. You might already have many of these items in your purse, and some of them you might not have even thought about. These items are must-have and recommended by many survivalists throughout the world.

This checklist is not exclusive by any means. Look at it, evaluate it, and find out what works best for you. Imagine if you were the woman in Oregon—what could you have done differently? Or picture yourself at your local grocery store, dropping your kids off at school or practice, or walking to your car alone at the mall. What would you do to stay vigilant and ready? What items could you have with you to protect yourself? Keep these questions in mind when you put your purse survival kit together.

In any survival situation, you must always think about food, fire, shelter, water, and security.

Communication Items

Communication and signaling are key components of survival, which makes a phone and charger essential.

A mirror can also be used as a signaling device. Send flashes of light from the mirror to attract attention.

You can also signal with smoke or fire, and if you carry a lighter, you'll have the means to make both. You can also make

Lighter

a fire for signaling, warmth, protection, cooking food, and dis-infecting water if necessary. The means to make fire is a necessity in every survival kit.

A bright scarf also can be used as a signaling device. Place the scarf in a highly visible position or wear it on your head to shade you from the sun.

A whistle can be used to signal as well. Use it to call for help while signaling your location to others.

Personal Protection

What would you want to have in your purse if you were in-volved in the attack scenario at the start of the chapter? Does pepper spray, mace, or a Taser come to mind? What about a knife or a gun? If you live in a state where it is legal and you can carry a weapon, are you trained and proficient in the use of a gun? Do you carry your gun with you, either on your body or in your purse?

We recommend carrying a pistol, but only if you have the proper training and necessary permits. A firearm in the hands of a trained person is an absolutely deadly weapon. Although warning shots should never be fired (you don't know where the bullet might end up; you don't want the bullet to hit something other than your intended target), a pistol can be very intimidating and could save your life from a would-be attacker. Of course, you need to have the requisite permit and training to carry a weapon and attain the concealed handgun license if your state has a concealed handgun license program.

You want to ensure your pistol is comfortable and easy for you to operate and conceal in your purse. It also must be easy to withdraw from your purse. You can purchase holsters specifically designed to fit purses as well as special purses that provide a holster for a pistol. There are many manufacturers of carry holsters, purses, bags, and other items that can conceal a pistol. Check reputable websites on the Internet or visit your local gun store and hunting or sporting goods store. Select the gun you are most comfortable with and that is easy for you to use.

You must practice and be proficient in the draw, loading, reloading, and operation of your weapon. Go to a range where you can practice these requisite skills. Practice drawing your pistol from your purse at the range. Find a good, certified firearms instructor to train you.

After you've got the basics down, a pistol becomes a viable option to protect yourself and your loved ones in a dangerous situation. Remember, these skills are perishable if they are not practiced and maintained. You want to achieve muscle memory

Personal Mace

Revolver and Holster

when you reach into your purse to draw your weapon and put it into use. Muscle memory means it does not require much thought—your body reacts to the situation and it knows what to do because you've practiced it time and time again. In an ideal situation, you will be assessing the threat or multiple threats, looking for a way out, looking for a safe area, and taking care of others in your party as you methodically and fluidly draw your weapon and prepare to defend yourself. Practice makes perfect.

If you can't carry a pistol or don't feel comfortable carrying and using one, there are other items you can carry to defend yourself. A kubaton is a compact key chain that can be used as a weapon, and a tactical baton, which is a hardened steel rod, can be extended and used to hit, poke, and swing at an attacker. The baton telescopes out and comes in various sizes.

Other items to consider are an umbrella and a walking stick. You could go James Bond style and include weapons in your walking stick, such as a handle that has a knife blade that extends into the shaft of the stick. Even if you don't go that route, a walking stick or an umbrella can be an extension of your arm that you can use to poke, swing at, or choke an attacker. Either of these items can give you some stand-off distance and you can do some harm to an attacker if you hit the person in soft target areas of the body like the eyes, nose, throat, or groin. This can allow you to defend yourself or buy yourself some time to get away.

Multitool

If you choose to carry a baton, keychain, umbrella, or walking stick, train with it. Know how to swing it, open it, and poke with it. Train on a human-sized dummy target and work on hitting the soft areas of the body.

You should also carry a small knife or multitool in your purse survival kit. A knife can be used as a weapon, but more importantly, it is a tool to cut, pry, open things, make things, etc.

Food and Water

You also want to have a water bottle and some snacks or energy bars in your purse survival kit. The bottle itself can be used to gather more water. Also include some form of nutrient-dense food such as nuts, seeds, dried fruit, or energy bars. Any of these would give you some energy if you need it in a tough situation.

First Aid and Shelter

Make sure you keep a small first aid kit in your purse. You may need to control and stop minor bleeding or protect minor scrapes and cuts. An ACE bandage, gauze for wounds, supplies to make a splint, and some basic over-the-counter medicines should be included. These items can fit in a simple food storage bag or small makeup bag.

An emergency space blanket should be included in your purse survival kit. It is small, lightweight, compact, and could

Umbrellas

Wrist
Compass

easily go in your first aid kit. The blanket can be used to reflect heat inward to keep you warm or to make a hasty shelter. It can also be used as a poncho to keep you dry in wet conditions.

Additional Supplies

You'll also want to include a wrist compass or small compass in your purse survival kit. A compass can help you find your way and keep you steering in the direction you want to go. Learn and know how to use and read a compass.

Cash can go a long way, so keep twenty to one hundred dollars in your kit. You can use this to get a cab and purchase other food, water, and survival items.

SURVIVAL TIP #1: KEEP COOL IN A SURVIVAL SITUATION

Your brain is your most powerful weapon in a survival situation. Keeping cool, calm, and collected can keep you alive.

When confronted by a life-or-death situation, remember to not lose it and stay calm. A calm, methodic, calculating mind will conserve energy and help you think through the predicament you are in. Stay calm and don't panic. Panic can render you helpless and ineffective. Think through a tentative plan. Evaluate whether your decisions are logical, and think about what your family, friends, and the experts would think of your decision making process. Here are some steps to make sure you stay alive and keep a level head:

1. **Take an Inventory of Yourself.** Are you still in a hazardous situation? If so, get out of the area and get to a safe location. Are you injured? If so, get out of danger and treat yourself as soon as you can. Stop any bleeding immediately. If you're not alone, is someone in your party injured? Are you fit enough to undertake any physical effort you are considering, such as a long walk for help? Can you physically do what you need to do to survive? Are you fed, hydrated, and rested? How long do you think can you go before you need water, food, and rest?

BASIC FIRST AID KIT

☐ Adhesive bandages of various sizes

☐ Gauze pads and a roll of gauze

☐ Tape (waterproof first aid tape or duct tape)

☐ Antibacterial ointment

☐ ACE bandage

☐ Aspirin or acetaminophen (Tylenol)

☐ Ibuprofen (Advil, Motrin)

☐ Diphenhydramine (Benadryl)

☐ Motion-sickness medicine (Dramamine)

☐ Epinephrine (EpiPen) if you have any severe allergies

☐ Emergency space blanket

First Aid Kit

2. **Take an Inventory of Your Gear.** What gear and supplies do you have with you? Inventory it—clothing, food, water, fire-starting equipment, shelter, and weapons. Are you

with equipment—a vehicle, plane, farm equipment, four wheeler, etc.? Do you have gas? Oil? Car seats with padding for warmth and to sleep on? Identify what you can use and feasibly carry with you if you need to move. In most survival situations, the experts recommend you stay with your vehicle or craft and wait for rescue. Do you have a cell phone? Signal mirror? Bright clothing with which to signal? Wood to make a fire and signal and keep warm and secure? Do you have a flare gun? A radio? Again, inventory your gear and see what can be of benefit to you.

3. **Make an Attempt to Determine Your Location.** Do you have a map? Do you know where you are? Are you in an area you've been to many times before? Do you have a GPS that works? Don't assume you can rely on your cell phone's GPS. Learn how to read a map and determine your position with resectioning, which is a method you can use to orient yourself using a topographic map and a compass. Take an orienteering course to acquire these important skills.

4. **Come Up With a Plan.** Methodically and logically determine what you are going to do. Are you going to stay in place? Are you going to attempt to get help? Do you have the gear and physical stamina to get help? Does anyone know you are gone and will someone be looking for you? Did you tell anyone your plans, where you were going, etc.? How long will you be out alone before anyone starts to wonder where you are and when you will return? These are all relevant questions to ask yourself when you are deciding whether to hunker down and wait for help or attempt to get yourself to outside help. After you've come up with your plan, think about it. Does it make sense? Is it feasible? Can you physically and mentally execute your plan? If there are others in your party, does your plan

make sense to them? Are you all in agreement? Do you have time to make adjustments to your plan? Remember, two heads are typically better than one.

5. **Execute Your Survival Plan.** When you decide to act, act decisively. If you decide to stay in place, do so. Improve your position, find water and food, protect yourself, and come up with a means to signal would-be rescuers. Is there a time when your location might no longer be tenable and you will need to eventually move? Make sure that is part of your plan. Are you going to move? What gear, weapons, equipment, and people will you take with you? Is everyone leaving? If not, what is the plan if you do not return? Have you communicated your plan to everyone who is with you? Do they understand the plan? If people are staying behind, do they understand the plan and the instructions you are leaving them? If you decide to move, what happens if you need to turn back? How are you going to mark your route? Can you navigate over the land with a compass and map? Do you have a good sense of direction?

These five steps will help you keep your "head in the game" during a survival situation. Think about contingencies, and understand that if things can go wrong they probably will. You need to be ready for anything and cover as many contingencies as possible.

Remember to stay calm, think things through, and DO NOT PANIC! What would a reasonable person do if she were in your situation? It is your job to take care of you—only you can control your emotions. Keep them in check and fall back on the things you know, the information in this book, and get out alive!

SUMMARY

Many women already carry some of the recommended pieces of a purse survival kit. These common items can be lifesavers in a survival situation. It's important to remember, though, that the gear itself isn't enough. You must know how to use it and practice using it to gain the maximum benefits. This is especially true of carrying a weapon. Seek out the training you need and practice regularly so you are ready. Practice situational awareness—always pay attention to what is happening around you. Who's near you? Where could a person be hiding out of sight? What are the potential threats? This will prepare you for any type of situation life throws at you.

PURSE SURVIVAL KIT

CHAPTER TWO

EVERYDAY CARRY KIT

THE SURVIVAL SCENARIO

Just after the New Year's Day 2013, moviegoers in a small town on Staten Island were allegedly robbed at knifepoint while walking to their cars.

According to court papers, three men approached the moviegoers, displayed a knife, and ordered them to hand over their cash and phones. The muggers then entered a nearby car and drove off with an alleged accomplice behind the wheel. According to records, this all happened in broad daylight at around 3:30 in the afternoon.

THE ANALYSIS

No one wants to be in this scenario. Imagine walking out of the movies or the mall and being accosted by a group of assailants, one of them armed.

What could the victims of this mugging have done? Were they focusing inward when they were walking to their vehicles or were they focused on their surroundings and trying to identify any threats or an area where a threat could occur? Did they try to defend themselves? Were they carrying anything that could be used to defend themselves? Did they have anything in their cars to defend themselves?

EVERYDAY CARRY KIT GEAR LIST

- ☐ Bike bag or backpack
- ☐ Cell phone
- ☐ Phone charger
- ☐ Water bottle
- ☐ Lighter or matches
- ☐ Food (energy bar or food bars)
- ☐ Light jacket or space blanket
- ☐ Wrist compass or mini compass
- ☐ Knife (Swiss Army or survival knife)
- ☐ Pistol (if you have a concealed weapons permit where you live)
- ☐ Kubaton, tactical baton, or walking stick
- ☐ Mace/pepper spray or a Taser
- ☐ Basic first aid kit

This scenario could happen anywhere. In this specific case it happened in Staten Island, New York, where it is illegal to carry a concealed handgun. If this happened in another state where there are licensed concealed weapons holders, would this still have happened? There are still muggings, robberies, and murders in every state, regardless of concealed weapons laws.

THE TAKEAWAY

When you're out in public, remain vigilant, focus on your surroundings and environment, and maintain situational awareness. Make sure you know what's happening around you. Carry yourself in this manner and be able to react to changes that may occur around you. Simply maintaining this mind-set and showing your awareness by your demeanor makes you less likely to be assaulted. The military calls this making yourself a "hard target."

In addition to being a hard target, it's important to carry gear for personal protection. The everyday carry kit list in this chapter provides numerous options that can help if you find yourself in a bad situation Of course, you must practice using any gear you choose to carry and master using it for the gear to be effective.

EVERYDAY CARRY KITS

An everyday carry kit is just what it sounds like—a survival kit that you carry with you at all times. When considering your everyday carry kit gear list, think about the environment you're in and the things you'll need in a survival situation–water, fire, shelter, food, and protection/security.

Timbuk2 Bag

Multitool

Compass, Lighter, Energy Bar, and Water Bottle

The items in this kit are a good starting point, but if there is something important to you that you have with you at all times, add it to your everyday kit. Also, give some consideration as to how you are going to carry the items in this kit. You may feel comfortable carrying these items on your person or in a coat with zippered pockets during the winter months. However, a backpack, messenger bag, or purse is a good year-round option.

Cover the Basics

You want to make sure you have a phone and charger with you at all times, a water bottle, a lighter or matches, and some food in the form of energy bars or snack bars. Remember, this is your everyday carry kit, so it does not need to be packed with tons of gear, but it still needs to have the basics. Make sure you have a light jacket or blanket in the kit, as well as a small compass, should you need to navigate through unfamiliar territory. A space blanket is a compact, lightweight sheet that will radiate most of your body's heat back to you.

Your everyday kit should have a multitool or Swiss Army knife in it. Remember, your knife is a tool and a weapon. Know how to use all of the attachments and accessories on the knife you choose to carry. Some have files, scissors, pliers, different screwdriver heads, and even small saws. Choose one you are comfortable with and you know how to use.

Security

Personal protection is a must. If you have the necessary permits and training, a pistol can be a great way to protect yourself. If you would prefer not to carry a gun, consider adding a walking stick or tactical baton to your everyday carry kit. See chapter one for more on using a tactical baton or walking stick for protection.

In this chapter's survival scenario, a concealed weapon was not an option. Consider what you will do when you plan to go into an establishment that doesn't allow a concealed weapon or

Springfield Armory XD Sub-Compact .40cal, Monkey Fist, and Walking Stick

knife. While having your weapon with you at all times is ideal, keep it as close by as possible, such as in your vehicle. It's better to have your weapon with you or very close to you and not need it than to not have it and need it. Mace, pepper spray, or even a Taser can subdue a potential threat and allow you enough time to get away.

Basic First Aid Kit

In addition to the items listed above, you need to have a small, basic first aid kit. This should include adhesive bandages of various sizes, antibacterial ointment, gauze, and tape. This kit should also have some basic medicines such as aspirin, ibuprofen, Benadryl, and motion-sickness medicine (Dramamine). If you or someone traveling with you has a severe allergy to bee stings or if you have any other severe allergies, you should include an EpiPen in the kit. Most of these items can be purchased without a prescription at any drugstore.

SURVIVAL TIP #2: GETTING AROUND WATER
Detour Bypass Method

This method is simply a series of 90-degree turns to avoid the water. Use this if you come upon a lake, pond, or swamp. Effec-

KITS WITHIN KITS

Use smaller containers to keep your everyday carry kit organized. Group like things together in a container to make a minikit within your kit. For example, use a separate container such as a resealable plastic bag, repurposed candy tin, or other small container for the items in your first aid kit. These minikits will help you stay organized while keeping these items easy to find.

Minikit

tive use of this method also depends on the size of the water. If you encounter an enormous body of water, this method might take a very long time.

To execute the detour bypass method:

1. If you can see the opposite shore, make note of any significant landmarks directly across from you. Keep these in mind and make them your navigational guide. When you get to those landmarks, you know you will have successfully navigated around the water and are continuing in your original direction of travel.

2. Turn 90 degrees from your direction of travel and walk parallel to the water obstacle. Count your steps as soon as you start walking.

3. When you reach the far edge of the water, make a note of how many steps you took. Then make another 90-degree turn and again walk parallel to the water until you reach the far edge. You do not need to count your steps.

4. At the far edge, make another 90-degree turn and walk parallel to the water. Begin counting your steps and walk the same number of steps that you took in step 1 to get to the first edge of the water. Keep an eye out for the landmarks you identified before crossing. If you are keeping a consistent pace, you should reach them after you've taken the same number of steps you walked in step 2. When you reach your landmark, make another 90-degree turn to put you back in your original direction of travel. You have now avoided the water by boxing around the water obstacle.

Rope Assist Crossing

If there are two or more of you in your party and you have a rope, you can use it to assist you in crossing the water. This method is especially useful for crossing a river, creek, or ravine and can help transport people and gear.

To execute the rope assist crossing method:

- The strongest swimmer in the group transports the rope across the water and secures it to some anchor point—a strong tree, log, rock, etc. *Never tie the rope directly to your body.* If the rope gets caught on something while you are crossing, the rope could drag you down and drown you before you could untie it. It is best to have a loop in the rope that you can put around your hand or wrist. If the rope does get snagged, you can just slide your hand out without risk of being pulled under the water.

- After the rope is secured and anchored, use it to pull across gear, people, etc.
- You can also anchor the rope on the near side of the water. Put a quick release in the rope, so when you are done and everyone and all gear is across, you can release the rope from the near side and pull it over to the far side of the obstacle.

Swim, Float, or Raft Across

If you are comfortable in the water and a strong swimmer, you can swim across a body of water. If you're not a strong swimmer, don't attempt it. Hopefully your gear or survival kit is waterproofed. Storing your gear in a simple plastic storage bag (or two or three of them) can make a pack fairly waterproof. If you have a survival kit, put it in a construction-grade trash bag to make it waterproof. Now you have a big flotation device to help you make the swim across the water. You can push it, lay on it, etc. If there are two or more of you, you can make a poncho raft with your packs and use the raft to help you get across. You can push the poncho raft, lay on it, and paddle across the water; both of you could push and kick across.

If you are not water confident, avoid the water at all costs. Take a swimming class and get confident in and around the water. Regardless of your age, you should learn how to swim and be comfortable in the water and learn basic drown-proofing techniques that are taught in many classes.Basic drown-proofing techniques include:

- Inflating your shirt and floating
- Inflating your pants and floating

Remember to relax and stay calm and still. Try not to exert a great deal of energy.

SUMMARY

Your everyday carry kit is the kit that is going to get you through everyday life. What can life throw at you each day going to and from work, from a kid's practice, to the store, or the movies? The items in the everyday kit can help protect you, get you through a bad situation, and make things more comfortable. Water, fire, shelter, food, and security should always be considered and included in your kit. Pack for and expect the worst and make sure you practice and are proficient with all of your gear. When and if the going gets tough, your everyday carry kit can help you get home or to a safer location.

CHAPTER THREE

HIP BAG KIT

THE SURVIVAL SCENARIO

The New York Post reported last year that Central Park had a higher rise in crime than the entire city of New York. It cited the widespread use of smartphones and tablets in the park as the cause. Many people in the park using these electronic devices are having them stolen. In one example of this type of theft, two attackers jumped a 46-year-old man who was carrying an iPad with him while he jogged. The attack happened at 6:15 a.m. As the man was being punched, he dropped his iPad and the muggers fled without taking the device.

THE ANALYSIS

What steps could be taken to prevent this from happening? The man who was jumped at the park was not practicing situational awareness. He likely was too engaged with his iPad to be aware of his surroundings. It's also an example of being at the wrong place at the wrong time. At 6:15 a.m., it was probably still dark out or just getting light, making it hard to see if there were any potential threats.

What kit could the jogger have had with him to ward off an attack and how could that kit be readily accessible? For New York City, carrying a pistol is clearly not an option due to laws that restrict carrying a concealed weapon. But that doesn't mean he had to be weaponless during his run.

THE TAKEAWAY

Think about what you do on a daily basis or on the weekends. Where and when do you walk your dog? When and where do you exercise? Do you often find yourself alone? Could you defend yourself if you had to during your daily routine? What gear would you like to have to make you more effective and more formidable against an opponent or group of assailants?

A hip bag kit is perfect for use during physical activities such as jogging, walking your dogs, or rock climbing. It contains gear that will help you protect yourself as well as practical gear you may need or want while you are out. What if you fall and sprain your ankle while running or walking? The basic first aid items in your bag can help you address any immediate bleeding and you can use your phone to call someone to pick you up if you can't walk to your final destination. Never go out empty-handed. Find a bag that is comfortable to use while you are active and fill it with the essential gear in this chapter.

When putting your hip bag together think about water, fire, shelter, food, and security. Always consider these survival basics when you are assembling your kit. How can you carry, find, and purify water, make a fire, construct a shelter, gather or kill food, and protect yourself? These considerations should be the basis for everything you do.

HIP BAG KIT

Gear for your hip bag is very similar to the gear found in the purse kit and everyday kit. Remember, this is a recommended starting point. Find what works best for you and what types of weapons are legal for you to carry in your area or your intended destination. For instance, when running in the mountains of Colorado, you may want to carry a pistol because you are con-

Hip Bag

cerned about mountain lions. When most of us go for a walk, jog, or hike, we are not concerned about wild animals attacking us, but what about getting assaulted? You have to find what is easiest to carry and deploy in a stressful situation. As with all gear, it's important to practice with the items in your kit so you know you can access and use them quickly and comfortably.

The Hip Bag

A hip bag is a bag that rests on your hip. The bag strap goes over one shoulder and around the hip to make it secure yet unobtrusive. Choose a bag that is comfortable, secure on your hip, and one that can carry all of the recommended gear.

Covering the Basics: Fire, Food, Shelter, and Water

In a bad situation, you want to make sure you have a way to start a fire, so pack matches and a lighter in the hip bag kit. Stormproof matches are relatively inexpensive, burn for up to fifteen seconds, and can even burn under water. Even though these matches burn in just about any conditions, you still want to make sure they stay waterproof in your kit. Create a mini fire-

Kel-Tec .380 Pistol, UDAP Pepper Spray, Monkey Fist

starting kit by storing the matches in a cylindrical case with an O-ring and screw cap that create a good seal. Food storage bags are another good option and can hold both your matches and lighter. As an extra precaution, put the minikit in a second food storage bag. Remove the air from the bags before sealing them. Place your loaded food storage bag into another food storage bag and remove the air as well. If one of the plastic bags fails or is punctured, you still have backup to keep your fire-starter kit dry.

You'll want to have a water bottle and a couple of energy bars or some nuts in your kit, especially if you've been active before encountering a survival situation. Select an energy bar that tastes good to you and that has a good balance of fat, protein, and carbohydrates. Don't go for a bar that is completely all carbohydrates and is full of refined sugar. A bar with fat, protein, and carbohydrates will sustain you and give you energy for a longer period of time.

Add a first aid kit that will help you deal with scrapes, cuts, and sprains. In addition to adhesive bandages, add gauze, alcohol swabs, antibacterial ointment, and elastic bandages.

A bandana, scarf, or handkerchief can also be used to wrap a wound. If you are severely allergic to bee stings, have an EpiPen in your kit. Add some over-the-counter medicines like aspirin or acetaminophen (Tylenol) for pain, ibuprofen (Advil, Motrin) for inflammation, and Benadryl for allergies. Visit your local drugstore and go to the travel-size section to find these items for your first aid kit. Store them in a plastic food storage bag to keep them waterproof and to make them easy to find.

Make sure you have your emergency space blanket and always carry some cash.

A space blanket is light, bright, and can keep you warm and give you some shelter and protection from the wind, rain, and cold. You want to make sure you have cash to get home, get a cab, and buy some supplies if necessary.

Also include a multitool or Swiss Army knife in your kit. Know how to use all of the attachments and accessories on the knife you choose to carry. Choose a knife or multitool you are comfortable with and know how to use.

Lighter and Stormproof Matches

SURVIVAL TIP #3: HOMEMADE FIRE STARTERS

Getting a fire started in a survival situation could mean life or death. A fire can be used to keep you warm, ward off dangerous animals, purify water, dry out wet clothing and gear, and cook caught or killed game. Most of all, a fire provides security and a sense of comfort and well-being. Remember the mental piece of survival: If you can give yourself some of the creature comforts of home when you are fighting for your life, it can give you peace of mind, calm you, make you think more clearly, and help you in a not-so-ideal situation.

Fire starters come in many different shapes and sizes, and you can make your own fire-starting kits at home. These are cheap, simple to make, and can help you get a fire started quickly whether you are in a survival situation or just out camping with the family. Here are a few homemade fire-starting devices:

Wooden Matches Dipped in Paraffin Wax

Dipping the matches in paraffin wax will help them stay waterproof in wet conditions. You can also put these in a waterproof match container with a rubber O-ring, then put the container in a resealable plastic bag or two. When you are ready to start a fire, scrape the wax off and you have a match ready to go.

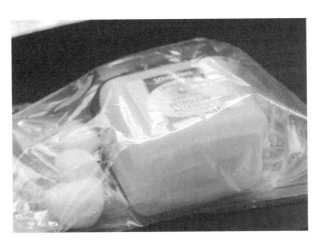

**Petroleum
Jelly-Soaked
Cotton Balls**

Cotton Balls Dipped in Petroleum Jelly

This is very simple to do. Just grab a handful of cotton balls and saturate them with petroleum jelly (Vaseline). These make a great fire-starting device. Put your cotton balls in a resealable plastic bag, and then reinforce them with another resealable plastic bag. When you are ready to start a fire, the petroleum jelly-soaked cotton balls can be used to get your kindling going. They will burn for a long time.

Dryer Lint, Egg Carton, and Paraffin Wax

To make this you will need a paper egg carton, dryer lint, and paraffin wax.

1. Lay your egg carton down in a well-ventilated space, preferably outside on your patio, on a workbench, etc.
2. Stuff each egg cup in the carton with the dryer lint.
3. Heat the paraffin wax until melted and pour it over the egg carton until both the carton and lint are fully saturated with wax.
4. Let the waxed egg carton cool until the wax hardens.
5. Cut the egg carton into pieces. One egg cup becomes one fire starter . You now have a dozen (or more) fire starters.

Keep these in a waterproof container until you are ready to use them. A waterproof container can be a resealable plastic bag or two. When you are ready to start your fire, remove one of the egg carton/lint/wax pieces. Light the piece on fire and you are ready to go. This improvised fire starter will burn for well over fifteen minutes. This is more than enough time to get a nice fire going.

SUMMARY

There are many everyday, affordable things you can use to create a fire-starting kit. Your imagination is the only limiting factor when it comes to survival and being prepared. Think about what works for you and what you are comfortable with. Be sure and practice on a regular basis with whatever tools and kit you decide to carry. This especially includes making and starting a fire. Practice with your fire starters in all conditions–cold, wet, windy, hot, dry, and snowy. You never know where you might end up. You want to prepare yourself to deal with any environment and overcome challenging conditions.

CHAPTER FOUR

POCKET SURVIVAL KIT

THE SURVIVAL SCENARIO

Summer months mean a rise in temperature and a rise in outdoor activities for many people in the United States. Many hikers strap on their packs and get ready to hit the trails during the summer. If history is an indicator, thousands of these hikers will need to be rescued. The search and rescue team at Yosemite National Park responds to three hundred incidents a year, nearly one a day.

THE ANALYSIS

Many hikers don't pack properly. They leave out essential items. Young and inexperienced hikers are the worst offenders. The most common reason for leaving out items is that a hiker intends to only go for a short summer hike. But too often, a wrong turn or sudden change in weather can turn a short hike into a long and ugly fight for survival.

The second most common reason for not packing items is simple forgetfulness. In a recent survey, only 9 of 167 hikers said that they did not own the unpacked equipment.

Perhaps another reason some hikers neglect to pack the necessary equipment is they believe they can rely on some form

POCKET SURVIVAL KIT GEAR LIST

- ☐ Pocket bag
- ☐ Cell phone
- ☐ Small signal mirror and whistle
- ☐ Pistol
- ☐ Pepper spray, Mace, Taser, or baton
- ☐ Knife
- ☐ Lighter or fire-starting device
- ☐ Emergency space blanket or poncho
- ☐ Wrist compass or mini compass
- ☐ Water and food

of GPS technology, usually a GPS-enabled cell phone, to aid in their recovery if something happens.

THE TAKEAWAY

When enjoying the great outdoors, you must be prepared and think of possible contingencies. When going for a day hike, you should have some essential items with you even if you think it is only going to be for a few hours. Experienced hikers know that cell phones will have little or no reception within a large park or vast outdoor space. Even dedicated GPS receivers sometimes fail. Ensure you have backup equipment in the form of a map, compass, and protractor.

Do a map study of the area you will be hiking in. Access Google Maps and check satellite photos to identify catching terrain features and landmarks to keep you on the right path. A catching feature is something you know you will run into when you have gone too far, such as a river, large creek, cliff, or gorge—something you identify that can help guide you and keep you oriented while you are out hiking in the woods. Also make sure you have a lost man plan, which is outlined at the end of this chapter.

POCKET SURVIVAL KIT

Just like the other gear lists, this list is not all-inclusive. What works best for you, your experience, and what you need for the environment you are in are key for packing the right gear.

Cell Phone

Even if you're in a remote area, your phone still might have coverage. If it does not have coverage, the lack of service might be intermittent, so you can still have a chance of using your phone in a survival situation. You can call for help, navigate with your phone, and keep a locator on your phone. When you leave your plan with someone you trust, make sure you tell them you will

Pocket Bag

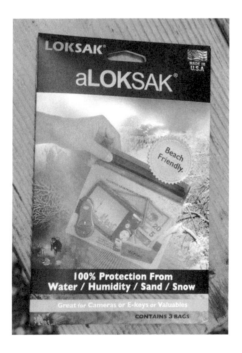

have your phone and have the locator on. Don't think all is lost if you don't have a constant signal. You still might be able to use your phone. On that note, conserve your battery power by powering down all applications. Also, to conserve battery power, turn your phone off when you're not using it. When you leave your plan with someone, establish tentative communication windows, or check-in windows. For example, you could tell others that you will contact them when you arrive at a certain destination and that this will take place between certain set times. Turn on your phone, make the call or send a text message, then power down your phone until your next check-in.

A phone should not be totally relied upon, but you may be able to use it in a survival situation.

Signal Mirror and Whistle

A signal mirror and whistle can be used to get the attention of others if you happen to get lost or injured.

Pistol

A firearm in the hands of a trained person is an absolutely dead-ly weapon. Never fire a warning shot. If someone or something is coming to take your life or injure you and you feel threatened with imminent bodily harm or death, do not fire a warning shot.

Heckler & Koch P2000 SK

Cold Steel Recon 1

A stray bullet could easily hit an innocent bystander and could land you in a lot of legal trouble.

Most people do not want to willingly take a person's life. But if it is you versus your attacker(s), you have to make a decision where you will prevail.

If you believe you are in a life-and-death scenario, aim for the center mass of your target and fire. Trying to shoot a disabling shot on a wild animal is not recommended as it will likely only enrage the animal further and not slow it down.

Pepper Spray, Mace, Taser, or Baton

A personal pepper spray fogger with a hand strap is great for a pocket survival kit. The right type of canister will put out a shotgun blast pattern of pepper spray. You know you will hit your intended target and slow down or ward off an attacker, which could give you time to get away and call for help. The range of some mace products is 10 to 15 feet (3 to 5 meters). This gives you a good buffer between you and your would-be attacker.

You can carry a Taser or tactical baton in your pocket kit if you are not comfortable handling a pistol or mace. A combination of these protective measures can be used, but this is a pocket kit and space is going to be limited. Think about what is going to work best for you and what you can rapidly employ to protect yourself.

Knife, Lighter, and Fire-Starting Device

No survival kit is complete without a knife and a fire starter. Make sure you have a Swiss Army knife, small knife, or multitool in your kit as well as a lighter and/or matches. You never know when you might need to get a fire going.

Emergency Space Blanket or Poncho

Have some protection against the elements like wind, rain, snow, cold, and heat. A small poncho or emergency space blanket can help protect you from all of these. It can help keep you warm, help cut the chill of the wind, and help keep the sun off if you use either one to construct an overhead canopy. A small poncho or a space blanket can easily fit into your kit.

Food and Water

Don't forget food and water. You can get an energy bar and an emergency water packet into a pocket kit. Some waist bags even have a spot for a water bottle attachment, which would be even better. We can survive without food for weeks, but water is an absolute necessity. The larger the container you can carry and incorporate into your kit, the better.

SURVIVAL TIP #4: PACK FOR THE ENVIRONMENT AND EXPECT THE WORST

When you go out into the woods, take a long trip, or just leave your home, make sure you are packing the right gear for the environment.

Do your research and find out what the weather will be like during the time of year you will be there. What is the terrain like? What navigational aids and catching features can you use? Do you have maps, a compass, and GPS to confirm your route and location? If you are taking a road trip, what are your primary and alternate routes? What is your plan if you have mechani-

Small Poncho

cal issues with your car? If you are you going to be traveling in a remote location, do you have a basic survival kit with you? Make sure your gear is appropriate to the season. You wouldn't want to pack a -20-degree rated sleeping bag if you're going on a day hike in the Davis Mountains in Texas in June.

METT+T Analysis

Consider your preparedness in military terms using this acronym: METT+T, which stands for Mission, Enemy, Troops and Fire Support Available, Terrain and Weather, plus Time and can be integrated with survival very easily.

Analyzing your hike, trip, etc., in these terms can and will help you better plan and prepare for what you plan on doing. This type of analysis will also help you plan for contingencies. Complacency can cause laziness and worse, death, if not confronted and dealt with. A thorough analysis will help you plan for not just one contingency but many. It will help you think through potential hazardous situations, problem areas, or things that will take you away from your original plan—weather, an injury, loss of communication, getting lost, etc. All of these are considerations you should be thinking about, assessing, planning for, and incorporating into what you plan on doing.

- **Mission.** Use the five Ws (who, what, when, where, and why), and how, to help you create a complete plan. Who is going on this trip? Are you going alone or are others accompanying you? What are the plans for your trip and what supplies are you bringing? When are you taking this trip? Where, precisely, are you going? Why are you going and what are your intentions? How are you executing this trip and what does this trip entail?
- **Enemy.** In terms of a day hike, the enemy can be dehydration, hunger, land navigation challenges, and difficult terrain. Make sure you can keep hydrated and replenish calories during and after the hike.

- **Troops and Fire Support Available.** Fire Support is for military but could apply in a survival situation. What weapons, gear, and ammunition do you have available to accomplish your mission? What—in the form of troops or neighbors, friends, relatives, and like-minded people—do you have to assist you in your mission? Will you have support available from park rangers and park staff? What about other visitors and campers at the park? Leave your plan with the park staff and family members and set a time for them to get or send help if you don't check in by a certain time. For example, if no one hears from you by 2:00 p.m., they should message you. By 3:00 p.m., they should try to contact you and make sure everything is okay. If they don't hear from you by then, they should send help or contact the park staff. This is assuming you have good cell phone coverage in the area.

  If you don't have reliable cell phone coverage there are a few things you can do: Speak to your cell phone provider and see where coverage is best in the area. Make sure you leave a detailed plan of your trip, including timelines, with friends, family, and park employees in the area you are visiting. Set up rally points on your route in case anyone gets lost and leave these with park employees/rangers. Do a thorough map reconnaissance to see where there is good, high, unobstructed ground to potentially get phone coverage. Check with the park personnel to see if there are towers, lookout points, cabins, or stations that you could navigate to in an emergency and get help. Turn your cell phone locator on so friends and family have the ability to track you. Even though you might not have any coverage or intermittent coverage, you still might be able to be tracked and use your phone as a backup for navigation. You can get a two-way radio, a satellite phone, and have a CB radio in your car. Satellite phones are very pricey; if money is no object, they can be an option. Many of us have gone to the woods with no phone and been fine. Make sure you plan your route, plan your exit, and know where safe areas and civilization are in case you have an emergency.

- **Terrain and Weather.** What is the terrain like? How can it affect you and those in your party—will it slow you down, speed you up, or beat you down? What are the conditions going to be when you are in that area? What is the forecast? What is the likelihood for severe weather while you are out? Are you prepared to deal with rapidly changing conditions? What is your plan to get out of the area if severe weather moves in? Where will you go? Will you hunker down? What will the weather to do you?

- **Time.** What is the timeline for your trip? Make sure you plan accordingly. What will you do if you do not adhere to your timeline? Is there room to be flexible? Is there somewhere you need to be where your timeline can no longer be flexible? Make sure you plan to pack your gear, do gear checks, confirm your route, mission, lost-man plan, injury plan, etc. Remember to adhere to your timeline and/or adjust it if you can be flexible.

Lost-Man Plan

You need to have a timeline and designated meeting place: If you get lost, return to the last known location where everyone was together, then return to the vehicle, or another designated meeting area, by a certain time. Try to communicate with others in your party if you can. If you don't reach the car by a certain time, everyone will know there is a problem.

If you do not have cell phone coverage and are missing a person in your group, keep the rest of your party together and don't separate. Stick to your designated meeting place(s), plan, and timeline. Everyone should know to return by a certain time.

If someone or a group does not get to the meeting place by the planned time the missing party may have a problem.

Injured-Man Plan

Treat yourself first, then anyone else in your party who is injured. If the injury cannot be managed by self-aid or a buddy, get help or call for help.

Try to use a phone if you can. You can also use your whistle and your signal mirror, depending on the time of day and your location. The whistle can be immediate. If you have a weapon, you could fire a shot or two in the worst-case scenario. Do not fire unless you definitely hear something; you don't want to waste ammunition if you can't get help.

SUMMARY

The thorough METT+T analysis can help you in any situation. Remember to think about what can potentially go wrong. A guy named Murphy once said that if things can go wrong, they will—it's just a matter of when. Have the right gear, the right plan, and the right training to take on the area. Plan for contingencies and think about what you will do to work through them. Never take things for granted. The weather can change and what you thought would be a bright sunny day might change in an instant. If you don't adequately prepare you could die out there. You need to be smart, fit, and sometimes mean, to persevere and get through hard times and situations.

CHAPTER FIVE

EMERGENCY 72-HOUR KIT

THE SURVIVAL SCENARIO

On New Year's Day, 2014, almost a foot of snow was forecast for the New York area, potentially snarling travel across the Northeast following the holiday. The storm was to give way to the coldest temperatures to date for the 2013/2014 seasons.

Two systems were forecast to merge, bringing as much as 10 inches (25cm) of snow to New York and 14 inches (36cm) to Boston, according to the National Weather Service. Snowfall started in the early morning hours and continued throughout the day.

THE ANALYSIS

In New York City, the worst of the storm affected the Thursday ride home. Most commuters weren't able to leave their offices on Thursday evening. Anticipating that driving conditions would deteriorate, the state closed several roads and expressways.

The storm affected more than 70 million people in the Midwest and Northeast combined and had a major negative impact on travel for people returning from holiday destinations.

EMERGENCY 72-HOUR KIT GEAR LIST

☐ Backpack

☐ Survival knife

☐ Signal mirror

☐ Multitool

☐ Survival whistle

☐ Lensatic compass

☐ Headlamp

☐ Breath of Life Emergency Escape Mask

☐ Emergency hand-crank radio

☐ Fire starters

☐ Water purification drops or iodine tablets

☐ Water bottle with filter

☐ Insect repellant

☐ Bathing wipes

☐ Basic Hygiene Kit

☐ Bug head net

☐ Bivy sack or tarp

☐ Poncho or some type of rain gear

☐ 550 paracord or some type of cordage

☐ Poncho/shelter combination

☐ Emergency food and water

☐ Bear spray or pepper spray

☐ Monkey fist

☐ Pistol with 120 rounds of ammunition

☐ Reference materials

☐ Maps

☐ First aid kit

THE TAKEAWAY

Be prepared for flight delays and cancellations because of direct and indirect impacts from a far-reaching storm. You may need to be prepared to stay at home, stay at the office, or stay in a hotel until streets are cleared and safe to travel. You need to be prepared to take care of yourself, and potentially, others if you are stuck in one location. At home, this should not be too much of a problem—you should be able to sustain yourself for more than a few days. If you are at work, traveling for work, or on a vacation this might prove more difficult if you are not prepared. Plan for contingencies all the time. During the winter months, expect storm delays, adverse weather, and delayed travel that could last for days. During thunderstorm season in the midwestern United States (hurricane season during the summer months), these events occur fairly regularly and should be part of your thought and planning process when you are in your home and away from it.

If you are away from home, you should bring a survival kit with you. What size, what configuration? How long should you be ready to weather the storm? We recommend a 72-hour kit. The Federal Emergency Management Agency (FEMA) recommends having a three-day supply of food and water as a minimum in your 72-hour kit. During most severe weather events, things typically wind down within a day or two but sometimes it takes longer to return to normalcy. Be prepared to either stay where you are or abandon your current location for longer if necessary; however, a 72-hour supply should be your starting point.

EMERGENCY 72-HOUR KIT

This is a bag designed to truly survive a 72-hour emergency event. You won't find any playing cards and chewing gum in this bag. This bag is designed for people who want to survive a true grid-down event such as an earthquake, tornado, hurricane, or other weather-related event. If you are in a survival scenario for more than three days, this kit provides six days of food for one person.

If you live in an earthquake zone, tornado alley, hurricane zone, or an area that has potential civil unrest, this is the bag for you. Leave nothing to chance, especially your life. Carry this kit in your car and bring it into your office on work days for a worst-case scenario. Have peace of mind knowing you can get through a bad situation and know you can hunker down in the office or anywhere else if you need to.

Backpack

Use a pack that can carry all of the recommended gear. Make sure your pack is hydration compatible, meaning that it can accomodate a water bladder. Also look for one that has lots of storage and is comfortable. You want to be able to access gear quickly and efficiently, so look for one with easy-to-access

72-Hour Pack

pockets on the outside of the pack. You also want easy access into your pack by means of a zipper, drawstring and clips.

Look for a military- or field-tested pack. Check manufacturer websites and blogs for what experts and laymen are saying about the pack you are considering. Go to your nearest outdoor, survival, or camping store and try out the pack for fit, user friendliness, features, and comfort.

Survival Knife

For the 72-hour kit you want a beefy knife. Make sure it is a knife that has a full tang blade. A full tang blade means that the blade and handle are one solid piece of steel. This makes the knife much stronger so it can be used to skin an animal, protect yourself, chop down trees, or make a spear. This is going to be one of the more useful tools you can have in the kit. Look for durability and quality.

Signal Mirror

Just like the compact that a woman carries in her purse, this mirror is something every survivalist and every person should have in their kit. You want a mirror that has a focus point where you can aim the mirror toward a target. The focus point will concentrate energy from the sun and send a nice bright flash as a signal. Look for a mirror that is small, lightweight, and compact, preferably one that's 2 to 3 inches (5cm to 8cm) in size.

Multitool

A multitool is a must in your 72-hour kit. Look for one that is versatile and has the following functions: needle-nose pliers, regular pliers, hard wire cutters, wire cutters, wire stripper, knife, serrated knife, saw, spring action scissors, ruler, can opener, bottle opener, wood/metal file, diamond-coated file, large bit driver, small bit driver, and a medium screwdriver.

Most multitools are small and compact and do not weigh much. A good multitool is perfect for any job, adventure, maintenance, or everyday task, and it can prove especially useful in a survival situation.

Survival Whistle

A survival whistle is another must in the 72-hour kit. It can be used for signaling to call for help, warn of danger, or to fix your position. By simply blowing your whistle, you can easily let people know of your position with minimal effort if you are injured

Survival
Whistle

and can't move or if someone in your party is injured. Other people will then be able to navigate to your location. Ensure you have a whistle that can generate a loud shrieking sound and can be operated when wet. A whistle is useful in any environment.

Lensatic Compass

A reliable compass is an essential piece of gear, especially in extreme conditions. Choose a compass that consistently works and is easy to read. Look for one with the following features: fixed declination correction scale, detachable snap lock in the lanyard so it's easy to work with the map, luminous bezel and markings for ease of use in low light and dark conditions, centimeter scale

Handheld Compass

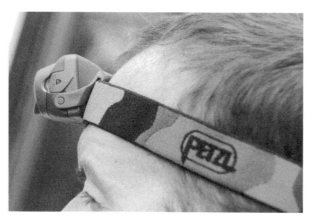

Headlamp

for measuring distances on a map, and a baseplate with magnifying lens. These features will help you orient yourself so you can move to a safe and secure environment.

Headlamp

Look for a headlamp that is lightweight, compact, and comes in a tactical model. The tactical version should have the option of a red lens filter. This lens can be used to preserve your vision when you are operating at night. You want to have a light with a strong, bright lumen white beam that allows you to distinguish between colors. Make sure the LED module is sealed, and look for a headlamp that uses AAA batteries and burns for over 100 hours at a minimum. There are headlamps on the market that are lightweight and can burn for 150+ hours on just three AAA batteries. The headlamp can obviously help you see at night and in low-light conditions. It can also be used when moving and operating in buildings with little or no light or as a signaling device.

Breath of Life Emergency Escape Mask

This pocket-sized, reasonably priced, lightweight, compact mask can be carried in a briefcase or pocketbook. It can be used to breathe in a burning building, where there is an airborne chemical irritant, and if the air is unclean. This is not a military gas

**Hand-Crank
Radio**

mask, but a mask that can help get you to a safe environment. It can give you 15 to 20 minutes of breathable air to get out of a bad situation. If you work in a city, a high-rise, warehouse, or very large office building, this mask needs to be in your pack.

Emergency Hand-Crank Radio

Make sure you get a hand-crank radio for your 72-hour kit. Either batteries or the hand-crank can power the radio, and the hand-crank can recharge the batteries. This is an essential piece of gear for your kit.

The radio should be good for AM/FM and weather bands. This is great on camping trips, for weather updates, and when there is a power failure, grid-down scenario, or some type of natural disaster. Your radio should also be able to receive emergency broadcasts. Some hand-crank radios not only charge the radio batteries but can also be used to recharge most common cell phones. Some additional features to look for when choosing your radio include a built-in 3 LED flashlight, digital clock with alarm, and thermometer with freeze alert.

Fire Starters

When choosing your fire starters, make sure you have some redundancy built in with multiple types of starters, including:

- **All-Weather Fire Starter.** Make sure you have an all-weather fire starter that can get a fire going in any and all conditions. Choose one that is reliable and can perform consistently if you are injured, cold, in high winds, soaking wet, and exhausted. Fire starters like the BlastMatch send a stream of sparks onto kindling material that can get a fire going. With a magnesium block with flint, you shave shards of the magnesium into a little pile and then use the flint to create a spark to ignite the magnesium. These are just a few examples. Choose ones you are familiar with and you know how to operate efficiently. You don't want to be reading instructions in the cold, wind, and rain trying to get a fire started.

- **Stormproof Matches**. These are very reliable, especially in a survival situation when you need fire for warmth, cooking, and making a signal fire. These matches are inexpensive and can burn in just about any condition, even underwater. Stormproof matches will burn up to 15 seconds. This is plenty of time to get your kindling going and get your fire started. When choosing these matches, the authors recommend a pack of twenty-five or fifty in your kit.
- **Fire Paste**. This flammable paste comes in a tube, just like toothpaste. You can squeeze a quarter-size amount, ignite it, and get a fire going. This is a great piece of gear to add kindling to and make your fire larger. It will burn well and will stay lit in adverse conditions.

Remember that having multiple fire-starting options is key. There is nothing wrong with throwing a normal lighter in your kit as well.

Stormproof Matches and Fire Paste

Water Purification Drops or Iodine Tablets

Water treatment-drop kits allow you to treat up to 30 gallons (113 liters) of water. Water treatment drops will kill pathogens in water and make it safe to drink. If there is a great deal of sediment or floating particles, filter the water first using a cloth, shirt, or cotton balls to remove the debris. Once the water is filtered, it's okay to treat. You don't want to be drinking a bunch of dirt and wood chips when you can make a quick filter. You just need to have a container to pour the water into your filtration material.

Iodine tablets can also be used to treat water. The iodine tablet is added to water and then you wait the instructed amount of time. The water is then typically safe to drink. There is the iodine taste to contend with so you could add some flavored drops or vitamin C tablets to the water to offset the taste of the iodine.

Both of these water purification tools can be found in a camping, survival, or outdoor store. They are light, easy to pack, have a long shelf life, and can be used to treat large volumes of water. Both are great for hiking, camping, hunting, fishing, boating, white water rafting, RV travel, home water storage, and emergency kits.

Aquamira Water Bottle with Filter

The Aquamira water bottle comes with a built-in filter. The filter will clear out pathogens and particles and make your water safe to drink. From one bottle, you can safely drink up to 5,060 ounces (150 liters), which is equal to about 40 gallons of water. This is a very valuable item to have in your kit. This filter is durable and can last a long time. In theory, you could use this to drink for 40 days, if necessary.

Insect Repellant

Make sure you have a repellant that offers long-lasting protection against black flies, ticks, chiggers, mosquitoes, deer flies, and other biting insects. There are many on the market. Put your repellant in a large ziplock bag so it does not leak into the rest of your gear.

Bathing Wipes

These are basic bathing wipes you would have in a diaper changing kit. You can use these on your hands, face, neck, armpits, genitals, and other areas of your body to remove dirt and grime. A little cut or scrape can turn into a big problem if not taken care of, and a rash from heat or fungus can make things very uncomfortable in a survival situation. Clean yourself daily. If you can't shower or bathe, use your bathing wipes to wipe down the areas described above, shave, brush your teeth, wash your hands, put on some powder, and you will feel brand new. You will be practicing good personal hygiene in a survival situation,

BASIC HYGIENE KIT

Men's Hygiene Kit

- ☐ Toothbrush
- ☐ Toothpaste
- ☐ Dental Floss
- ☐ Razor
- ☐ Shaving Cream
- ☐ Tweezers
- ☐ Fingernail Clippers
- ☐ Medicated Powder
- ☐ Lip Balm
- ☐ Sunscreen

Women's Hygiene Kit

- ☐ Toothbrush
- ☐ Toothpaste
- ☐ Dental Floss
- ☐ Feminine Products
- ☐ Tweezers
- ☐ Fingernail Clippers
- ☐ Medicated Powder
- ☐ Lip Balm
- ☐ Sunscreen

which will ensure you keep going for a long time and don't get sick. Don't let a small wound fester and grow into something that can't be managed or treated with basic first aid and good hygiene skills.

Basic Hygiene Kit

Your basic hygiene kit should be appropriate to your gender and you don't need both unless you are packing a 72-hour kit for a man and a woman. Also, think about including some type of medicated powder or antifungal cream. Both of these can be useful in a hot, humid environment. Medicated powder can also be used as foot powder and cooling powder in the armpits and on genitalia.

Bug Head Net

Another inexpensive lightweight piece of gear is the bug head net. This is useful when you will be sleeping outdoors to keep mosquitoes, bugs, and pests away from your head and face when you are trying to rest. It is simply an over-the-head bug protection net.

Bivy Sack or Tarp

Make sure you have something to keep you out of the elements such as a bivy sack or a tarp. A bivy sack is a thin-shelled, waterproof zippered bag you can crawl into for shelter and warmth. You can sleep in it and it will keep you warm and dry. You can put your sleeping bag inside a bivy sack for more protection and insulation from the weather. Look for a bivy sack that is lightweight, waterproof, and has easy access. Also, make sure if you plan on using it with your sleeping bag that it is large enough for you and your sleeping bag to fit inside.

A tarp is another option and can be fastened into a shelter. It will not offer the benefits of a good bivy sack; the tarp is going to be heavier and you might have to sacrifice gear to carry your

Bivy Sack

tarp. A large tarp and a bivy sack are close to the same price point, so opt for the lightweight bivy sack.

550 Paracord

You can have 550 paracord in your bootlaces to use in a survival situation. There are now survival bracelets made from durable 550 paracord that have fishing equipment integrated into the bracelet. This and/or some type of cordage that is strong enough to lash down gear, branches, or a tarp is something your 72-hour kit should have. This can be found at most survival, camping, and outdoor stores.

Poncho/Shelter Combination

This is another option to get you out of the elements that is very lightweight and easy to carry. This is exactly what it says it is, a poncho/shelter combination. It be worn as a poncho or constructed into a shelter by closing the hood and hanging the poncho off the ground to make a roof. Many military personnel do this with their military-issued ponchos. There are eyelets in the corners of the poncho that you tie rope/cordage to and then you can anchor the poncho.

Emergency Food and Water

Water packets and nutrient-dense bars are what you get with the Emergency Food and Water brand. The package can provide you with up to six days or more of food in the form of bars and water packets. You are going to need water and nutrients. Emergency Food and Water is lightweight, compact, and can fit into your pack well. This is another great addition to have in your 72-hour kit.

Bear Spray or Pepper Spray

The key here is to select a spray that disperses the most active ingredients in the shortest amount of time. There are many products on the market, but look for one that can get the ingredients out quickly and with high volume. The spray can be used on a bear, person, or an angry or unruly mob that is after you. Make sure you are upwind when you disperse the spray so you don't incapacitate yourself when you are trying to ward off an attack.

Monkey Fist

A monkey fist is a dense ball of 550 paracord formed around a ball bearing. It has an attached lanyard with a loop that you can fit around your wrist. A monkey fist can be used as a weapon to hit an attacker and it can be used for what it was originally designed and intended for: to add weight to the end of a rope to be able to throw it into an area. It was developed in the Navy and is still used today to heave lines for mooring to a pier, ship, vessel, or object. In a survival situation, if you are not on water, you can use it to throw lines over trees, across water, etc.

Monkey Fist

Pistol with 120 Rounds of Ammunition

This might not be something you can keep in your office or something that can be attached to your hip at all times. A pistol should be part of your 72-hour kit and you should have at least 120 rounds of ammunition. This is something that can save your life, ward off would-be attackers, kill game, and protect others in your party. It is essential that you refer to your local regulations for carry laws and rules about having a firearm in your possession.

Reference Material

One recommended book for every large survival kit is the *SAS Survival Handbook*. This handbook covers a wealth of information from fire starting, constructing a shelter, food gathering, edible and poisonous plants, cleaning an animal, basic land navigation, and celestial navigation. You can even get the book in a waterproof version. Anything and just about everything you can think about for survival is covered in the book. We can't retain everything, so it is an excellent reference tool to have in your 72-hour kit.

Maps

Make sure you have maps of the local and surrounding areas. Don't rely on Google Maps and your phone. Look for street maps, topographical maps. Make sure you have maps of potential locations you might need to travel to and from. Many outdoor stores and gas stations have maps of local areas, and they're inexpensive.

First Aid Kit

You need to have a first aid kit in your gear. You can get a prepackaged kit with many types of bandages, gauze, sterile dressings, gloves, moleskin, and over-the-counter medicines. Make sure it has these supplies so you can treat cuts and scrapes, sprains, headaches, muscle aches, allergic reactions, and larger wounds.

SURVIVAL TIP #5: TAKE A BASIC FIRST AID AND BASIC LIFE SUPPORT COURSE

There are many courses you can take to better prepare you for a survival situation. Something that is often overlooked is first aid and basic life support skills. With first aid in a survival

BUGGING OUT AND BUGGING IN

In survivalist circles, the term "bugging out" basically means abandoning your current location (often your home) due to a natural or human-caused disaster. "Bugging in" means hunkering down in your current location for survival. In either scenario, you have to make sure that you will be safe and will have enough supplies to survive. We cannot predict when or where a problem will occur, but we can control how prepared we are to meet a survival situation when it comes.

situation there will probably be a time when triaging the wounded, sick, and dead will more than likely be necessary. Will you be prepared to do all or any of those things? A basic first aid course is a good place to start.

If you are out in the woods, you or someone in your party should have these skills. Asthma inhalers and EpiPens should be in a survival kit as well.

SUMMARY

Your emergency 72-hour kit needs to be right for you and the environment you are in. Plan for contingencies, the weather in your area, and an ever-changing, chaotic situation. Make sure you have the things you need for 72 or more hours and that you have the tools to go well beyond that so you can get home to your family and loved ones.

CHAPTER SIX

URBAN BUG OUT KIT

THE SURVIVAL SCENARIO

On Thursday, August 14, 2003, just before 4:10 p.m. EST, a software problem in Ohio caused the Northeast blackout of 2003. This power outage affected areas of the northeastern and midwestern United States and the Canadian province of Ontario. Nearly 55 million people lost power, and many were without power for days. We don't expect this to happen, especially in America. It has been quite some time since something like this has occurred, but there are power surges that happen daily. The summer months can cause a huge strain and drain on power. Will you be prepared when the power goes out the next time?

THE ANALYSIS

Imagine yourself in one of the major metropolitan areas affected by this blackout in 2003. What would you have done? Would you have been one of the people walking across the Brooklyn Bridge? Would you have extra food, water, and a means to communicate? Without a communication device, how would you link up with your family and loved ones? These are things to think about. How would you accomplish these things?

6

URBAN BUG OUT KIT GEAR LIST

☐ Pack

☐ Knife

☐ Breath of Life Emergency Escape Mask

☐ Dry bag

☐ Duct tape

☐ Fire starters

☐ Survival whistle

☐ Wrist compass

☐ Headlamp

☐ Water bottle with filter

☐ Poncho

☐ Bivy sack

☐ Insect repellant

☐ Bathing wipes

☐ Personal hygiene kit

☐ Bug head net

☐ Food and water

☐ Bear spray or pepper spray

☐ Survival manual

☐ Maps

☐ First aid kit

☐ Pistol with 120 rounds of ammunition

THE TAKEAWAY

The ability to communicate and stay informed during emergency situations is key. A shortwave radio with a hand crank could allow you to follow information and updates. The kit in this chapter includes other items that will help keep you up and running or hunkered down until things return to normal. You also need to have a link-up plan in place that you've practiced with friends and family members. Sit down with the people you care about and come up with ideas on where you can meet, a timeline, and contingency plans if your initial and secondary meeting points are unreachable. When you practice and rehearse your plans, make sure you do it with the gear that will be on your back—the urban bug out kit.

URBAN BUG OUT BAG

The bag should not be so heavy that you are not mobile and not effective. This kit keeps your bag lightweight and will allow you to move swiftly, silently, and stealthily.

Many of these items have been covered in the previous chapters, but the focus here is on how they can be used in an urban environment. Remember, the gear you are the most familiar with and most comfortable with is the gear that is going to work the best for you in a survival situation. You don't want to learn how to use things when you are in an already bad or grim situation.

The Pack

Make sure your pack is hydration capable, has lots of storage, and is comfortable. You want to be able to access your gear quickly and efficiently, and that calls for easy-to-access pockets on the outside of the pack. You also want easy access into your pack by means of a zipper, drawstring, and fastek clips.

A military- or field-tested pack is best here. Reputable blogs, websites, and experienced friends or colleagues can help you get started. Always try out the pack for fit, user friendliness,

SELECTING A SURVIVAL PACK

Look for the following when choosing a survival pack:

- **Access Panels.** How will you get in and out of the pack? Look for a pack that has vertical zippers that open the front of the pack, allowing you to rapidly load and unload the contents of your pack. Choose a pack that has internal compression straps to keep stress off the zippers and secure your load. Look for a pack that can also be loaded from the top. A pack with different compartments separated by a zipper or drawstring allows for quick loading and unloading of the pack from the top or bottom.

- **Radio Pockets.** Radio pockets are positioned against the pack's frame for safety and stability and are capable of carrying a multiband radio. Ports are also provided for antenna and communication wiring. They are obviously useful for a radio and heavier gear that you will want to keep at the top of the pack.

- **Sternum and Load Stabilizer Straps.** A sternum strap is essential for keeping shoulder straps in the proper position. Look for a sternum strap that can be removed and repositioned on the shoulder straps. This makes the sternum strap adjustable, making your pack form-fitting. Also, look for an elastic section on the strap. This will allow for chest expansion during heavy exertion. Load stabilizers on the upper shoulder straps and on the hip belt keep heavy loads tight on the back. A hip belt also allows some of the pack weight to be loaded on the hips.

- **Crisscross Strap Closure.** Under the lid, look for a pack with straps that cross from the front to the back, and from side to side. These straps secure the load and provide extra lashing options. The side-to-side strap can neatly secure the side lift handles under the lid for extra snag-proof security. The side-to-side strap can also support the load of a water reservoir if you choose to have a water bladder of some sort in your pack.

features, and comfort. This is a bag you are going to pack with your urban gear and should not weigh more than 20 pounds (9 kilograms). You want to be quick and mobile, and ready to react in any situation. A heavy load on your back will make this tough to do.

Knife

For the urban bug out kit you want a knife with a full tang blade. A full tang blade means that the blade and handle are one solid piece of steel. This makes the knife much stronger, which means it can be used to skin an animal, protect yourself, chop down trees, pry open doors, and break into and open up places. Look for a good quality knife that can accomplish these things to include in your urban bug out kit.

Breath of Life Emergency Escape Mask

A pocket-sized survival mask will help you breathe clean air so you can safely escape a burning building or chemical explosion. See chapter five for more on survival masks.

Dry Bag

No one knows what the elements are going to throw at you, so waterproof your kit. A strong waterproof bag made of soft rubber will not only keep your gear dry but also provide a protective barrier against things that could poke or tear your pack. When moving in an urban environment you could encounter debris such as rebar, exposed sharp metals, beams, light posts, or ripped-up cars. Any of these could snag you or your pack and tear things open. A rubber waterproof bag will give you added protection to keep your gear safe and dry.

You can also use trash bags to waterproof your gear. Use at least two and secure the top of each one with a rubber band. Simply pack your gear in the inner trash bag, seal it by twisting the top and forming a gooseneck (just fold the wound part over on itself like a gooseneck, then secure it with a rubber band). Make sure you press all of the air out of the bag. Repeat this two to three times with more trash bags. The extra bags will provide extra protection and an extra barrier to the internal bag that holds your kit. Continue to gooseneck each subsequent bag and secure the top with a rubber band for easy access. If you tape the bags shut, you will ruin the bag each time you have to go in and get your gear. Therefore, use rubber bands and practice getting in and out of the bags to retrieve gear. You should be able to access your gear with and without light. Be sure to practice with whichever waterproofing method you use to ensure you are prepared.

Breath of Life Mask

Duct Tape

Duct tape is an essential piece of gear for any kit or situation. Use duct tape for first aid, including covering and compressing wounds, repairing things like clothing, latching down items, making an improvised weapon, sealing a leaky water bladder. A must for your urban kit, you can pick up a roll of duct tape just about anywhere.

Fire Starters

Make sure you have a way to start a fire, make sure you have more than one option for starting a fire, and make sure you have some type of cube or paste to act as kindling once you get a spark or flame going.

The Sparkie does exactly what the name says: It sends out sparks to ignite tinder and get a fire going. You can even do this using one hand, which can be useful in windy conditions: One hand can hold down the tinder and the other can operate the Sparkie to ignite it. The Sparkie is lightweight and slightly larger than a house key.

Duct Tape

WetFire Tinder Cubes come in a pack of eight and will help get a fire going. It is hard to get tinder going when it is wet or damp, but you won't have that problem with WetFire cubes. They burn very hot and long and burn even longer when they are wet. The WetFire Tinder Cube looks like a very dense marshmallow and can easily fit in your kit.

Survival Whistle

Refer to chapter five for the use of a whistle and its importance. A survival whistle is still very useful in an urban environment and can be used to signal, mark your position, provide early warning, and signal a coordinated movement such as an attack or retreat.

Wrist Compass

A compass is key for finding direction. If the city you are in is your hometown, navigation should not be a problem, but if you are traveling in an unfamiliar urban environment, a compass will be very useful. If you move underground or plan on moving at night, you will need a compass. A compass will be able to easily give you cardinal directions (north, south, east, and west), but be aware that the high concentration of metal in urban settings could cause a compass to not read exactly as it should.

Headlamp

Make sure you have a good headlamp in your urban kit. Chapter five offers more detail on the necessity and benefits of a tactical headlamp. Look for a headlamp that is lightweight, easy to use, and can last a long time. Make sure you have a flashlight or penlight as a backup. A large office building in the middle of the day will be completely dark inside. You will need something that can provide adequate light to move in the urban environment. A headlamp, flashlight, or penlight light will allow you to navigate through buildings, homes, and subways.

Water Bottle with Filter

Water Bottle with Filter

We can go without food for weeks, but we can only go without water for three days. Having a water bottle, and drinking from it, ensures you stay hydrated. Make sure you have the supplies to get you through six days. If you find yourself in a bad scenario, a bottle with a built-in filter will make water safe to drink and you won't have to carry around multiple water bottles or bladders of water. Water can get very heavy very quickly if you decide to carry too much.

Poncho

This is a totally waterproof piece of gear that can be worn, made into a lean-to, or used as a ground mat. The poncho itself is waterproof, but anywhere there is a hole or opening water can get through. This is your full-body raincoat that you can use during inclement weather and use to construct a hasty shelter. Ponchos are very inexpensive and should definitely be a part of your kit.

Bivy Sack

Another great piece of gear to keep you warm at night is the bivy sack. The bivy sack can be as useful and invaluable in an urban environment as in any rural area. Use it to sleep in and get warm quickly when the weather gets bad. It will keep you warm, dry, and help reflect your body heat inward for a comfortable, toasty night. See chapter five for more on bivy sacks.

Insect Repellant
There are bugs in the city, so it's better to have some bug spray than not. Make sure you have a repellant that offers long-lasting protection against black flies, ticks, chiggers, mosquitoes, deer flies, and other biting insects. Put your repellant in a large zip-lock bag so it does not leak into the rest of your gear.

Bathing Wipes
Keeping yourself clean will help prevent problems with infections and will keep you at your best in a survival situation. See chapter five for more details on bathing wipes.

Personal Hygiene Kit: Men
The personal hygiene kit should be appropriate to your gender. You don't need both unless you are packing an urban kit for a man and a woman. Also, think about including some type of medicated powder or antifungal cream. Medicated powder can also be used as foot powder and a cooling powder in the armpits and on genitalia.

Bug Head Net
Another inexpensive lightweight piece of gear is the bug head net. This is useful when you will be sleeping outdoors to keep mosquitoes, bugs, and pests away from your head and face when you are trying to rest.

Food and Water
You'll want at least a six-day supply of food. Select the best food and water options for you. Be cognizant of the weight of

these items. This is for your urban kit and you want to be fast and light on your feet. You want to be able to move quickly, efficiently, and with minimal effort. Don't pack tons of food. Energy bars are small, compact, and nutrient dense and will give you the calories you need without taking up too much space in your pack. You could also pack a mix of bars, dehydrated food (this is fairly lightweight), and an MRE (meals ready to eat) or two, but remember, a heavy pack will just slow you down.

Bear Spray or Pepper Spray
Look for a bear or pepper spray that can get the ingredients out quickly and with high volume. The spray can be used on a bear, person, or an unruly mob that is after you. Make sure you are upwind when you disperse the spray so you don't incapacitate yourself when you are trying to ward off an attack.

Survival Manual
One recommended book for every large survival kit is the *SAS Survival Handbook*, which will provide useful information on a variety of survival topics. See chapter five for more on this valuable resource.

Maps

Don't rely on Google Maps and your phone. Make sure you have maps of the surrounding areas and maps of potential locations you might need to travel to and from. Many good outdoor stores have maps of the local areas. Gas stations also have inexpensive roadmaps.

First Aid Kit

You need to have a first aid kit that can help you treat cuts, scrapes, larger wounds, sprains, headaches, and allergic reactions. A prepackaged kit will have all the supplies you need.

Pistol With 120 Rounds of Ammunition

If you have the proper training and necessary permits, a pistol can save your life, ward off would-be attackers, kill game, and protect others in your party. It is essential that you refer to local regulations for carry laws and firearm possession.

SURVIVAL TIP #6: CREATE CACHE SITES

A cache site is a concealed location where can you store your gear for resupply and replenishment. Concealment is key. You don't want someone to be able to find your stash of goodies. It needs to be well hidden but very easy for you to find and recognize. Even your backyard can be a good cache site. Other possibilities include parks, abandoned buildings, and waterways such as rivers, lakes, ponds, or streams. Make sure your kit is waterproofed and includes a drying agent if you are storing your kit in a damp environment.

If you are using your cache to store weapons, metals, batteries, and ammunition, be sure your cache is waterproof. Weaponry should be lubricated and bagged before it is stored. You can purchase waterproof storage containers in various sizes and shapes. You can also make your own. You can make your own with trash bags, large PVC tubing, a box, or wooden crate.

Make sure you waterproof your items with trash bags, ziplock bags, and tape or rubber bands and include a drying agent inside the storage vessel to get rid of moisture. An old saltshaker filled with rice can help capture moisture from within your self-made cache system.

Once you determine where you are going to place your cache and if you are going to have one or multiple cache sites, create a map—whether it's a mental map, paper map, or some type of code that only you know—to locate your gear. Navigate to each of your caches to restore your supplies. This will cut down on the load you have to carry when you are en route to your bug out location.

SUMMARY

Find and adopt the gear that works best for you, the gear you can afford, the gear you are well-trained to use and can operate from muscle memory and with your eyes closed. Always consider the environment you will be in and think about what you can feasibly carry on your back for a long period of time.

CHAPTER SEVEN

DAY HIKE KIT

THE SURVIVAL SCENARIO

You decide to go on a basic day hike alone in the local national forest close to where you live. You have been to this location many times before for simple one-day excursions. You start your hike at 8:00 a.m., following your normal trail. Right away, you notice things are very green and parts of the trail are overgrown. After a while you realize the trail is getting harder to follow. You know you are walking up and the gradient seems to be increasing, so you are pretty sure you will be up to your normal picture point soon. You look at your watch and realize it is almost 11:00 a.m., much later than your anticipated arrival time. You try to get a signal on your smartphone to get a fix on your location, but you don't have a signal. You turn around, but all you see is dense vegetation and you can't make out any trail at all.

Dark clouds are rolling in and you can feel the temperature has dropped at least 10 degrees. You remain calm and come up with some sort of plan to get yourself back to your car. You see what you think to be an open, higher area through the trees and begin to move to that location so you can get a better vantage point and get your phone to work. As you are moving you encounter a small creek that you are going to try and jump. You

DAY HIKE KIT GEAR LIST

- ☐ Pack
- ☐ Emergency water
- ☐ Water bottle
- ☐ Emergency drinking straw or water purification tablets/drops
- ☐ Poncho
- ☐ Emergency bivy sack
- ☐ Space blanket
- ☐ Cordage or 550 paracord
- ☐ Duct tape
- ☐ Fire starters, lighter, stormproof matches, WetFire tinder cubes, cotton balls, or homemade kindling (egg crate and lint as discussed in chapter six)
- ☐ Phone
- ☐ Compass
- ☐ Signal mirror
- ☐ Whistle
- ☐ Flashlight/headlamp
- ☐ Basic first aid kit and personal hygiene kit
- ☐ Insect repellant and insect head net
- ☐ Bear spray/pepper spray
- ☐ Emergency food
- ☐ Compact fishing kit
- ☐ Animal snare kit
- ☐ Knife
- ☐ Maps of the area
- ☐ Survival cards
- ☐ Survival manual if not too heavy

are moving faster now and getting worried because you begin to hear thunder in the distance and the temperature keeps getting cooler. You make your jump at the bank, but the near side is soft and you lose your footing. You not only fall into the creek, but you roll your ankle. You get up and try to gain your composure but find it is very hard to put weight on your ankle. Then you realize your phone was in your back pocket when you jumped and it was in the water for a while. Pretty soon you find yourself shivering a bit. You can still see what you think is an open area on the higher ground. You realize you are lost, cold, hear a storm rolling in, have no means of communication, and you are injured. What do you do now?

THE ANALYSIS

None of us wants to find ourselves in the situation of the lone hiker above. What are some of the things she did wrong? What gear should she have brought with her on what she thought was a normal day hike? Did she tell anyone where she was going? Did she bring any gear to protect herself from the elements or to communicate and navigate? Did she have anything for shelter or to construct a shelter? What about basic first aid supplies?

THE TAKEAWAY

Don't be caught out in the woods unprepared and let Mother Nature get the best of you. Make sure you have a basic day hike kit with you at all times, even if you are going to the same place you've been one hundred times. What should your day hike kit consist of? This chapter will cover the basic items you need to get yourself out of a potentially hazardous situation.

THE DAY HIKE KIT

When putting together your basic day hike kit, think about the basic necessities in a survival situation: shelter, water, fire, food, and security. Your day hike kit should go in a basic backpack, over-the-shoulder bag, or fanny pack. Remember, this is a day hike kit. You are not preparing for a long hunting or camping expedition. Your day hike kit could be on the outside of your ultimate bug out bag or your expedition pack. If you are in a base campsite and need to go out to hunt or gather food and water, you can detach your day hike kit and take it with you. Your kit will still have all of the necessary supplies to get you through a tough situation.

Much of this kit has been discussed and covered in previous chapters. Rather than reiterate those items of the kit, this chapter will focus on the relevance of these items in your day hiking kit.

Pack

The day pack should be smaller than your normal large backpack. It should be comfortable, tough, have a spot for a water bladder, and be large enough to accommodate all of the recommended items for a day hike. If our lost hiker would have had a pack with the appropriate gear, she might not have wound up in such a poor predicament. As discussed before, your pack needs to be the right one for you. Try out several and get the pack that is comfortable and the most functional and appropriate to what you are doing.

Day Pack

Emergency Drinking Straw

Water

If your pack has a pouch for a water bladder, get a bladder that fits your pack that also allows you to comfortably carry the largest amount of water possible. This is very important in more arid climates and during the summer months. In addition to having the water you brought along in your bladder, also bring water purification tablets or drops, a water purification straw, and a water bottle. A bottle with a built-in filter would work well here. The hiker above could have filled her bottle(s) or bladder at the creek and either filtered it or used purification tablets or droplets. Remember to stay ahead of dehydration. If you get injured, you are going to need even more water. Like other survival gear, you want to be redundant and have many options to gather, filter, and purify water.

Shelter

The hiker needed to have some form of shelter with her. She could have used a poncho when it started to rain and if she did not make it back to her vehicle she could have used a space

blanket or bivy sack to get through the night. Not only would these items help keep her dry, but they would also help reflect body heat back inward. It was getting colder, she was wet from the fall in the creek, and it was starting to rain. It is one thing to be cold and one thing to be wet, but worse to be cold and wet.

Some cordage, rope, or 550 paracord can help secure any shelter material you have. Duct tape can also prove useful to repair ripped or torn gear or clothes and it can be used as a first aid item to cover wounds, apply pressure, and construct splints.

Fire Starters

Fire-starting devices and fire-making tools are mission-essential pieces of gear. Don't leave home without them and don't forget to have them in your pack. A basic lighter, stormproof matches, magnesium stone, and some kindling material are all key items to have as fire starters. The bottom line is you need have something that can create a spark or flame and something that can burn easily to help you get a fire going, especially in the worst

550 Paracord

conditions imaginable. Getting a fire going will help you stay warm and dry out (with an adequate shelter). A fire can also give peace of mind and comfort.

Communication and Navigation Devices

You need to be able to move, communicate, and shoot if necessary. More importantly, you need to be able to move deliberately, i.e., get to where you want to go without getting lost. You'll need to have an understanding of land navigation, map reading, studying the terrain for the best route, and using these skills to get where you need to go with minimal effort. If you don't know how to navigate without the use of your phone or GPS, get additional training so you can. A phone and GPS are luxuries at best in a survival situation. You want to be a master of the basics when it comes to many survival skills, especially land navigation.

Communication is going to be necessary with your family, loved ones, friends, and the people you are working with or going to. You can communicate with smoke, fire, whistle blasts, fireworks, light during the day and night, and other things. Make sure that your communication plan is understood by everyone you are working with, and rehearse your communication plan.

- **Phone**. A cell phone can be your most valuable piece of gear if you have a signal and you can let someone know where you are so they can help you if you are lost or injured. If there is a grid-down scenario or you are simply in an area that has no coverage, you are out of luck. Do not rely on your phone as the only means of communication. You may have to get creative, so make sure your alternate communication signals are easy to understand. Always make sure you let someone know where you are going and what you are doing if you go out in the woods alone and give them your tentative time of return.
- **Compass and Map of the Area**. Learn how to read a map and use a lensatic compass. Don't rely on technology because your phone or GPS device might not work in a survival situation. In fact, count on it not to work and be ready to use a map and compass. Master the basics of map reading, orienteering, and land navigation. Don't assume you know the terrain like the back of your hand. Use a map, compass, terrain features, and land navigation aids to confirm what you are doing in terms of your route and movement.
- **Signal Mirror**. A signal mirror needs to be in your day hike kit. The signal mirror flash can be seen for miles and can attract attention to your location if you can't get a fire going.

Small Flashlight

- **Whistle.** The whistle can be used for signaling and to fix your position. The hiker could have used a whistle to call for help and to draw rescuers to her location if she was seriously injured.
- **Flashlight or Headlamp.** If you are out during the hours of darkness and plan on being able to move, some form of light is necessary. A flashlight or, preferably, headlamp is a must in this situation. A headlamp frees your hands for other things. A headlamp is a lightweight, affordable, easy-to-use piece of gear that needs to be in your day hike kit.

Basic First Aid Kit and Personal Hygiene Kit

A basic first aid kit with an ACE bandage or two, gauze, adhesive bandages, antibiotic cream, aspirin, Benadryl, sunscreen, and bandages is a good place to start. There are many affordable first aid kits on the market that can be a good addition to your day hike kit. Don't forget basic hygiene supplies as well. These have been mentioned in chapters five and six.

Insect Repellant and Insect Head Net

A good insect repellant can keep the bugs away and can keep you more comfortable if you are out for a day in the woods.

Bug Spray/
Insect
Repellant

Look for some of the repellants that have sunscreen as this can save you some weight in your pack.

Bear Spray/Pepper Spray

These personal defense items can be used to ward off a bear or mountain lion attack. Keep this on the outside of your day hike kit so you can access it immediately, if necessary. Make sure you are familiar with the operation of the type of spray you choose to carry.

Food

You want to make sure you have some food with you and you have the means to get food. You want to stay fresh and keep your mind sharp in a survival situation. The only way you can do this is by keeping good fuel in your tank. Nutrient-dense foods are key—nuts, seeds, and energy bars that have a balance of protein, fats, and carbohydrates. Make sure you include some food in your kit so you can refuel and keep going. Glucose is what powers the brain. If you are hungry and have not had any sugar (carbohydrates) for days, you are not going to be able to make the best decisions and problem solve. Making decisions, problem solving, and thinking clearly can save your life. Don't forget to pack some food!

- **Emergency Food.** Make sure you have some type of compact, calorie-rich food in your kit. Typically the best option is energy bars. See chapter five for more on emergency food.
- **Basic Fishing Kit.** If you find yourself in the woods longer than you expect, you can put your kit to use for fishing or catching crawfish. A compact fishing kit should have line, hooks, a bobber, and weights.
- **Animal Snare Kit.** Just like the fishing kit, an animal snare kit is a compact kit that can be used to snare small animals. Make sure you practice making snares and ensure

BASIC FISHING KIT

☐ Two rolls of fishing line

☐ Three bobbers

☐ Five lead weights

☐ Ten hooks, various sizes

☐ Emmrod Pack-Rod casting fishing pole,

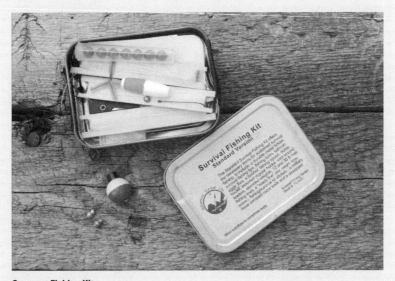

Compact Fishing Kit

you can find a good anchor point for your snare. Look for game trails, animal signs, and places where small animals are likely to move. You can set out some bait using some of your emergency food bars, then lay your snares around the bait, covering all likely areas of approach. Set out multiple snares to increase your chances of snaring an animal.

• **Knife.** Make sure you choose a full-tang blade when you purchase your knife. You can certainly have more than one type of knife in your day kit. See chapter five for more on full-tang blades.

Reference Materials

Have a map of the area and the surrounding areas you will be operating, moving, and hiking in. Make sure you know how to read the maps.

Survival cards are waterproof plastic cards that usually come bound together. They can help you with knots, how to start a fire, how to construct a shelter, how to find water, and many other important survival topics. These cards are valuable quick-reference guides that provide many helpful survival tips.

SURVIVAL TIP #7: TAKE A BASIC LAND NAVIGATION COURSE

The ability to land navigate is a skill everyone should have. You don't have to be a Boy Scout or member of the military to take a land navigation course. Some of these courses are held for free at outdoor stores. Also, check your area state and national parks for weekend programs on navigation. Such courses often

Reference Materials

cover how to use a compass, read a map, navigate with a map from point to point, find your position, shoot a magnetic azimuth, and gain familiarity with adjusting for magnetic deviation when navigating. The best courses offer classroom instruction and include some form of practical application so you can get outside and practice your skills. As you learn the basics, use your map and compass as your primary means to navigate, then use electronic devices to confirm your location. These skills and the right kit will help you be more confident in the outdoors and can help you rescue yourself and others when the unexpected happens.

SUMMARY

This list is not exhaustive for the day hike kit. These items are recommended and have been field tested time and time again in the civilian and military worlds. Add to or take away from the gear list, but you always need to think about water, shelter, fire, food, security, communication, land navigation, and first aid.

CHAPTER EIGHT

EMERGENCY CAR KIT

THE SURVIVAL SITUATION

The headlines in the winter of 2006 were dominated by the tragedy of the Kim family, who spent six days huddled in their car in the Oregon wilderness. At that point, the father, James Kim, decided to set off in search of help. Two days later, his wife and two daughters were found alive in the family car. Sadly, Mr. Kim's body was found two days later.

THE ANALYSIS

What happened to the Kim family is a heartbreaking tragedy that serves as a powerful reminder of the need to always be prepared to face a survival situation. What could the Kims have done differently? Having the right gear in the car could have helped them get through this awful ordeal. It's also important to remember to anticipate the weather you may encounter. Study the route you will be traveling and stick to the main highways and thoroughfares during adverse conditions. Side roads, short-cuts, and less-traveled roads are the roads that will be cleared last, if at all. Better to stay on a major highway and close to gas stations, stores, towns, and cities. If you get in trouble you can call or signal for help, but you are less likely to encounter other travelers on a side road. Stick to busy roads in bad weather; it may be slower and more tedious, but you don't want to get lost and turned around in bad conditions. Bad can go to much worse very quickly.

THE TAKEAWAY

If the Kims had an emergency car kit with a beacon, it could have proved helpful. Even without the beacon they could have still survived with extra clothing, fire-starting material, extra fuel to retrace their route, and food and water to help them get through the worst of the storm. In many survival situations, it is best to stay with your vehicle or mode of transport, especially if it is well equipped with gear to sustain you and keep you alive

EMERGENCY CAR KIT GEAR LIST

- ☐ Hip pack, tool bag, or something large enough to fit your gear
- ☐ Case of bottled water
- ☐ Water purification drops or tablets
- ☐ Emergency food
- ☐ Poncho
- ☐ Heavy blanket (preferably wool)
- ☐ Bivy sack
- ☐ Duct tape
- ☐ Cordage
- ☐ WetFire Tinder Cubes
- ☐ Stormproof matches
- ☐ Multitool
- ☐ Compass
- ☐ Light

until help arrives. The emergency car kit will help you weather a storm, an accident, mechanical failure, and aid you in getting help and staying warm, dry, well fed, and hydrated.

EMERGENCY CAR KIT

The items listed in this kit are a good place to start and build upon. Pack your kit according to the environment you are in or will encounter. For instance, if you are going to be driving through south central Texas in the middle of summer, you won't need four sleeping bags. Regardless of the weather, you will definitely need water, some type of water container, water purification, and fuel. From there, you will need to consider other items appropriate to the area, season, and terrain you are traveling in and through.

- ☐ Pepper spray
- ☐ Insect repellant
- ☐ First aid kit
- ☐ Ice scraper
- ☐ Help/emergency sign (reflective material)
- ☐ Road flares
- ☐ Fix-A-Flat
- ☐ Basic tools (pliers/adjustable wrench/flat head and screwdrivers)
- ☐ Motor oil
- ☐ Fuses
- ☐ Car-safe spare fuel
- ☐ Cell phone and charger
- ☐ Radio or CB
- ☐ Beacon

Pack

You want a hip pack that can carry and hold most of the kit. Although it is recommended that you stay with your vehicle, if you need to move, you'll have a bag that you can carry your kit in. The limitation for how much gear you want to have in your emergency car kit is up to your imagination and the size of your vehicle. Consider how much space you need in your trunk, seating area, or storage areas on a daily basis. From there, you will know how much room you have available for your emergency car kit. If you travel a lot for your job and you are in your car all time, you might want to stock up more than the average Joe who just drives to and from work, the grocery store, and the movies. If you might get stuck in your car for days, you want to have food, water, fire-starting material, warm clothes, and some security items in your kit. Make sure your emergency car kit is right for you, the environment you'll be in, and your hip pack.

Emergency Water and Food

If you can fit a case of bottled water in your vehicle, put one in there. In addition to the case of water, have some water purification tablets or drops so you can still make water drinkable if you go through the case of water. Save the used water bottles to collect water from rain, creeks, streams, lakes, ponds, or

Car Bag/Pack

potholes. If you can carry a filtered water bottle, put one of those in your emergency car kit as well. Redundancy with your gear still applies here. In fact, it applies even more for car kits because you are packing the gear in your vehicle, which allows for more room for these extra measures.

Have a supply of food that can last a minimum of three days. The food needs to be calorie dense and, if needed, can be stretched for as long as six days. Energy bars, nuts, seeds, trail mix, soup or broth, and jerky are all good options. You can even pack some dehydrated food. You should have some extra space in your vehicle and you won't be putting everything on your back unless you have to move, so make sure you have a good supply of food and water.

Shelter

Make sure you have a poncho and heavy blanket, preferably a wool blanket. Wool blankets are durable, they wick away moisture, and they keep you warm even if they are wet. Also, have a reliable bivy sack, a large roll of duct tape, and cordage in your car kit. You might have to construct some type of makeshift shelter if you can't sleep in your vehicle. Again, it's better to have than be without, especially when the gear is in your vehicle and you are not necessarily hiking or carrying it around.

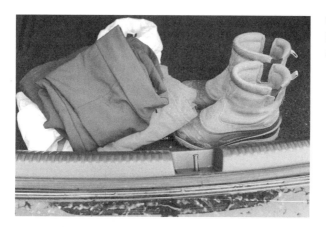

Wool Blanket,
Extra Clothes
and Boots

Matches and
WetFire Tinder

Pack some extra clothes, especially during the winter months. If you have to go out and forage and survey the area in the rain or wet snow and get drenched, you want to have something dry to change into, including extra socks, pants, shirt, an extra coat, boots, or shoes.

Fire Starters

Make sure you have fire-starting tools in your kit. You can also start a fire with the cigarette lighter in your vehicle and use the battery leads to make a spark. You also have combustible items in your vehicle: gas, oil, lubrication, interior insulation, carpeting, and seat padding. These are all good items to use as

fire starters and kindling. Still, pack some reliable stormproof matches and WetFire Tinder Cubes in your emergency car kit. The matches will give you the flame to get a fire started and the WetFire Tinder Cubes will burn and allow you to add more fuel to the fire. Both of these or items similar to them should be in your kit. Think about what the Kims could have done if they could have built themselves a roaring fire to stay warm, melt snow to drink, and give them security and piece of mind.

Security Items

A good multitool, compass, a light in the form of a headlamp or flashlight, pepper spray, insect repellant, and a first aid kit are necessary items for your bag. All of these can be used in a survival situation even if you are with your vehicle.

Vehicle-Specific Items

You'll also want to have items in your car that will make being in the car easier and safer when driving.

- **Ice Scraper.** This is a good tool to have if you'll be traveling in areas with ice and snow during the winter so you can keep your windshield clear. Think about where you live and where you will be traveling, then pack your vehicle according to those environments.

- **Shovel, Snow Chains, Salt and Cat Litter.** If your car wheels are stuck in snow or mud, these items will help you dig out and add enough traction to your tires to keep moving.
- **Help/Emergency Sign.** Make sure this sign is made of reflective material. Even a reflective triangle stored in a cylindrical tube can help notify passersby that you need assistance. An emergency sign can also be used on the road or on the roof of your car to signal for help. Aircraft will be able to see a brightly colored emergency sign on the roof of the car. If you put the sign on the roof, create as much contrast between the roof and sign as possible.
- **Road Flares.** Flares not only signal and warn other drivers

Fix-A-Flat

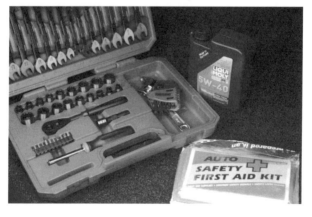

Motor Oil,
Tool Kit,
and First
Aid Kit

of upcoming danger, but you can also use them to start a fire and signal for help. The smoke and light generated by a flare can be seen and spotted from long distances.

- **Fix-A-Flat.** If your spare is wrecked and you are in the middle of nowhere, you can't get your jack to work, you are in unforgiving road conditions and you can't safely change the tire, or you get multiple flat tires, this is the option for you. Use the Fix-A-Flat to get the tire inflated. Also be sure to include a bright-colored reflective vest. If you are moving along the roadway in the middle of the night or have to change a tire along the side of the road, you want to make sure you are seen. This is an inexpensive piece of gear you can throw into your kit.
- **Basic Car Tool Kit.** This kit should consist of common tools you would use on your car. You won't be able to fix anything if you don't have the necessary tools, so keep them in your emergency car kit. Before any long trip, make sure you get your car serviced or checked out by a professional. Make sure everything is in good working order. If this is something you can do on your own, even

Jumper Cables and Handsaw

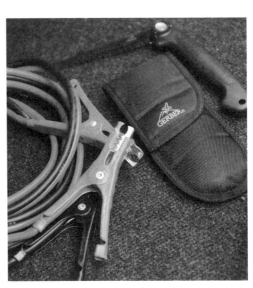

better. When checking your fluid levels, make sure you have the right amount of motor oil, antifreeze, and windshield cleaner, and make sure your battery is not dried out. Keep some extra motor oil and antifreeze in your emergency car kit. Again, do the right preventive maintenance and make sure you are checking your fluid levels before and during any long distance travel.

- **Fuses.** Don't get caught in horrible conditions in an unfamiliar environment and be stuck because you blew a fuse. Some cars have a space to store fuses by the fuse box. Storing the fuses common to your vehicle in the glove

BASIC CAR TOOK KIT

This minikit should include any items you might need to work on your car, including:

- ☐ Car jack
- ☐ Lug wrench
- ☐ Pliers
- ☐ Adjustable wrench
- ☐ Flat-head scewdrivers in various sizes
- ☐ Phillips-head screwdrivers in various sizes
- ☐ Motor oil
- ☐ Antifreeze
- ☐ Windshield cleaner
- ☐ Oil filter
- ☐ Replacement belts
- ☐ Spare hoses
- ☐ Fuses

compartment or center console is a good idea. Any auto store can tell you what fuses to get specific to your vehicle.

- **Jumper Cables.** You can use jumper cables to start your own vehicle or someone else's, and you can use them to create a spark to start a fire. You can keep them in the trunk, in your Emergency vehicle kit pack, or in the tool-box of a truck.
- **Handsaw or Small Wood Saw.** Should you need to remove a tree or other obstacle in the road, a saw will allow you to clear a path so you can continue.
- **Spare Fuel.** You don't want to run out of gas in a remote location and be stuck. Spare Fuel is a safe alternative to carrying gas in your car. The product is to be used when you run out of gas. You just pour it in your tank and start up your car. You will get the same mileage with Spare Fuel as you do with regular gasoline. A gallon is a must in every emergency car kit.
- **Additional Car Gear.** Since you have more room in your car, you may also want to include a small cooking stove, as well as an emergency power inverter to charge items like a cell phone.

Communication

A cell phone with car charger, CB radio, and an emergency beacon can potentially save your life if you are stranded in a remote location. Just about everyone carries a phone and keeps a charger for their phone in their car. However, a CB radio is another option, especially for long, cross-country trips. Both of these options will allow you to communicate, check weather or road conditions, and call for help if needed. An emergency beacon, if you can afford it, should be in your car kit. Just like a concealed weapon, you might never need to activate your beacon, but if and when you do, you don't want to be without it.

SURVIVAL TIP #8: DON'T GO IT ALONE

If possible, don't do things alone when you are in a survival situation. There is power in numbers, and two heads are often better than one. It is good to have someone to watch your back, bounce ideas off of, as well as to use each other as support.

Ideally, there will be someone like-minded and with a similar skill set with you. Better yet, their survival and preparedness skills complement yours. Try to train together. Practice shooting, land navigation, hiking, camping, and preparedness exercises together. You want to develop your communication skills with your partner or team. Learn how to anticipate each other's moves and begin to rely on one another just like you would in a real survival situation. Many have survived being alone, but it certainly helps when there are others involved.

If you are going to go it alone, make sure you let someone know what you are doing, where you are going, what your anticipated time of return is, and what to do if you don't make it back by your estimated time of return. Plan for contingencies when you are out alone. Let someone else know your intended route if you are traveling or if you are camping or hiking in the woods. Make sure the information you leave behind is easy to understand and your tentative route is easy to follow.

SUMMARY

Our modes of transportation are often taken for granted. We assume our vehicles are going to be reliable and get us to and from our destinations daily. As someone who is preparing for and expecting the worst, your vehicle is a great option for you to add an extra layer of protection against the unexpected. Sacrificing a little trunk space can have you outfitted and ready for any situation. With some ingenuity, imagination, and your emergency car kit, you and your vehicle will be ready for anything that gets thrown at you.

CHAPTER NINE

VACATION SURVIVAL KIT

THE SURVIVAL SCENARIO

In January 2014, a suspected outbreak of norovirus caused the illness of nearly seven hundred crew and passengers aboard a Royal Caribbean cruise ship. Many people were confined to their cabins, sick with gastroenteritis, which can cause vomiting and diarrhea.

THE ANALYSIS

Unfortunately, this isn't the only incidence of widespread illness on a cruise ship. You need to be prepared should you fall ill while traveling. A week of anticipated fun can quickly turn bad when living in close quarters with hundreds of people, or eating food and consuming drinks your body is not accustomed to. Amenities we take for granted like clean running water and food that is safe to eat and fully cooked are not always available in other countries.

THE TAKEAWAY

You need to study and prepare for where you are going to travel so you don't fall ill or get lost in a city or foreign country. You also need to review some of the local customs and how your

VACATION SURVIVOR KIT GEAR LIST

For Carry-On Bags

- ☐ Personal locator beacon
- ☐ Cell phone (fully charged)
- ☐ Water purification drops or tablets
- ☐ Water purification drinking tube
- ☐ Water bottle
- ☐ Medications [prescriptions, aspirin, Benadryl, ibuprofen (Advil, Motrin) or acetaminophen (Tylenol), antinausea medication (Dramamine)]
- ☐ Sunblock
- ☐ Outlet converter
- ☐ Small compass

For Checked Bags

- ☐ Backups of all the carry-on bag gear
- ☐ Language translator
- ☐ Whistle
- ☐ Personal protection
- ☐ Weather-appropriate clothing
- ☐ Compass
- ☐ Maps of the destination
- ☐ Cell phone charger

hosts live. The survival kit will provide you with all the items you need to safely return from vacation, even when difficult situations arise.

THE VACATION SURVIVAL KIT

When prepping your vacation survival kit, it's important to consider which items you can pack in your carry-on bag or luggage and get through security. The vacation survival kit covered in this chapter will work for carry-on luggage and checked bags.

Personal Locator Beacon

This is a pricey piece of gear, but well worth it. The emergency beacon has a transponder signal that links to satellites. When the device is activated, search parties are notified and can find your location anywhere in the world. You can be in the middle of the ocean, desert, or jungle and a rescue party will locate you.

Cell Phone

Make sure you start your travel with it fully charged and you have your charger with you. If you are traveling to an area that does not support a 120-volt outlet, bring an outlet converter. Keep your phone in a waterproof bag if you are in and around water and keep a protective case on your phone. Your phone can obviously be used to call for help if you have a satellite signal. You might not always have a signal, but if you move into the range of one, you want your phone charged and working so you can call for help.

Water

Assume that any water in a third-world country is tainted and not safe to drink. Make sure you are only drinking bottled water and use the bottled water to brush your teeth and wash any local fruits and vegetables you eat. If you have to drink from a faucet, use your water purification drops, tablets, or drinking tube before drinking the water. Likewise, if you are on a cruise ship and the water on the ship is deemed unsafe to drink, you need to be able to purify the water so it's safe to consume. If you wind up out in the ocean, remember these items will not filter out the salt. You will have to acquire water by other means, for instance, by collecting rainwater with your water bottle or another container. Nalgene bottles are excellent water bottles to have in your kit. They are a bit large, but you can carry them on a plane. Just fill them up with water once you get through security. You could also pack a water bladder like a Platypus in your kit. You could fill this with water from water bottles or a water fountain. Do you need to purify rainwater in order to drink it? No, you do not. You can capture it in a container and drink it. You could route water with your poncho into the large mouth of a Nalgene bottle and have water to drink.

**Water
Purification
Supplies**

Medications

If you are taking any prescription medications, get them filled before you leave for the trip and make sure you have more than enough should your trip be extended for any reason. Take all medication with you in your carry-on luggage. Also bring the following: aspirin for headaches, pain, and altitude sickness; Benadryl for any allergic reactions; acetaminophen or Ibuprofen for pain caused by pulls, strains, sprains, or more severe injuries; antinausea medication to help with motion sickness or food you may eat that does not agree with you. Store these medications in small, labeled plastic storage bags. You can put the meds in little plastic storage bags that are 3" × 2" (8cm x 5cm), then put all of the individually stored medicines in a large resealable sandwich bag. Storing your medication this way will keep it waterproof when you need it.

Sunblock

Have a small tube of sunblock in your kit. Getting a sunburn is not only painful, it can be dangerous. Select a sunblock with at least an SPF of 30 that includes UVA/UVB protection. Ideally, you want your sunblock to be both waterproof and sweatproof. When water is a limited resource, you want to keep your skin covered and protected as much as possible to prevent further fluid loss and dehydration. Make sure you have enough to reapply as needed. Also, don't forget about your lips. Pack a lip balm that has some sunscreen in it, preferably a minimum SPF of 15.

Small Compass

Since space is likely at a premium in your carry-on bag, select a small compass. Better yet, wear a wrist compass and use that limited carry-on space for something else. You could also consider including a button compass, which is a clip-on compass with a little hook that you can attach to your pack/bag or belt. It is always better to have more than one of the things that are in your kit.

Checked Bag Gear

If you are checking a bag, you will have room for some additional items that will be available to you in an emergency situation.

Have a duplicate set of the gear you have in your carry-on bag in your checked bag. Building redundancy into your survival gear will help you stay safe. If you can afford it, this also includes a personal locator beacon. If owning two beacons exceeds your budget, keep the one you have in your carry-on bag. Other items to include in your checked bag include:

- **Language Translator.** Although English is spoken in many countries, you want to follow the local customs. Do as the locals do and try to keep a low profile. If you have a smartphone, consider downloading a translation app. Otherwise, a book will do. Don't be the ugly American when you are abroad. If locals see you are trying to speak their language and you respect their customs, you will be received well and locals will be more likely to help you should the need arise.
- **Whistle.** Pack a whistle for signaling and communication. You can pack a metal whistle or a JetScream survival whistle. Both can produce a high-pitched sound. They are both very durable.

Spanish-
English
Dictionary

- **Personal Protection.** It is not advisable to travel with weapons of any kind, especially a firearm. You might be able to get by with a basic small knife, but be sure and check the laws before trying to bring a weapon into a foreign country. If needed, you can purchase a knife at a local store once you arrive at your destination. Make your trip through customs as painless as possible and remember to declare any weapons you purchase when you return to the United States.

- **Appropriate Clothing.** If you are going to London in December, don't pack for the tropics. Make sure you have an adequate amount of clothing, including some backup items appropriate to where you are traveling.

- **Compass.** You can have a larger compass in your checked bag. You can have a wrist compass and a larger compass like a Silva ranger or a Suunto handheld compass.

- **Maps of the Area.** Use the Internet to study the geography of the region you'll be visiting, including any places you might be traveling to on tours or excursions. This is a simple, yet integral, part of your preparedness and planning for travel to a new location. Plan your days, your routes, and know how to get back to your hotel. If you get separated from a tour party, you want to be able to find your way back.

- **Extra Cell Phone Chargers and Adapters.** Have a few additional chargers with the adapters for the area you are visiting. Most smartphones and phones are sold worldwide, but it is best to travel with what you know works and what you are familiar with.
- **Numbers to the Local American Embassy.** Program the local phone numbers to your hotel, tour guide, local police, and emergency, and especially the local American Embassy into your phone prior to your arrival in a foreign country. This can be done with minimal effort and time.

SURVIVAL TIP #9: STUDY THE LOCAL CUSTOMS WHEN TRAVELING TO A FOREIGN COUNTRY

As previously mentioned, you should do a map study of where you are traveling and where you plan on going when you get there. You should also study local customs before you get to a foreign land. A basic understanding and appreciation for these differences can lead to being accepted into a different culture and can also lead to a more rewarding vacation. Do your research on where you are going. A great place to start is The

CIA's World
Factbook
Webpage

World Factbook page, found on the CIA's webpage at www. cia.gov/library/publications/the-world-factbook/index.html. This site can give you great information on most countries, including political information, geographic data, the state of the economy, and more. This is a valuable tool to use to get you ready for your trip abroad.

SUMMARY

All items in this survival kit should easily get through security and will lend you a peace of mind. You can add to this list, but remember, most airlines are charging more for checked bags. Even though the survival kit is small, compact, and lightweight, you will still need to be prepared in case disaster strikes. In addition to your gear, as mentioned, study the area you are traveling to and see what additional vaccinations you might need and what medication you might need to take. For example, you should take malaria medicine when traveling to a mosquito-infested area. Make sure you practice good hygiene by washing your hands, eating food that is thoroughly cooked, and only drinking bottled water. Learn about the customs of your destination so you are better prepared and you can have a safe, enjoyable trip.

CHAPTER TEN

STUDENT SURVIVAL KIT

THE SURVIVAL SCENARIO

Tragically, it seems as if each school year brings a new headline about violence at schools. The 2012 shooting at Sandy Hook Elementary School and the 2007 shooting at Virginia Tech are grim reminders that students face dangers even in school settings. Thirty-two people were killed and seventeen others wounded during the Virginia Tech incident.

But it's not just violence students must be prepared for. A winter storm that hit Atlanta in January 2014 forced hundreds of young students to spend the night at their schools.

THE ANALYSIS

Both Sandy Hook and Virginia Tech were awful tragedies. Students in high school and below are limited by law, age, and maturity level in what they can safely and reasonably carry for personal safety, but they can still be prepared.

College students have more options available. What could some of the Virginia Tech students have had in their packs to help them get away, escape, and protect themselves and others in this active-shooter situation? Most college campuses do not allow a student to carry a firearm to class, but are there other

STUDENT SURVIVAL KIT GEAR LIST

- ☐ Pack
- ☐ Phone
- ☐ Phone charger
- ☐ Emergency contact list
- ☐ Water bottle
- ☐ Granola bar
- ☐ Emergency whistle
- ☐ Emergency blanket (such as Heatsheets)
- ☐ Comfort item
- ☐ Sweatshirt and extra change of clothes

Additional Kit Items for College Students:

- ☐ Breath of Life Emergency Escape Mask
- ☐ Pepper spray
- ☐ Forcible entry tool

things they could have had to help? Yes, and that's what you will find in the student survival kit.

While everyone was safe during the Atlanta winter storm and staying in place was the best option for many schools, you can imagine how uncomfortable and possibly scared many of those children were as they were forced to spend the night away from their families and homes. What could the students' parents have sent their children to school with that would have provided comfort and warmth, both physically and mentally, during the sheltering-in situation?

THE TAKEAWAY

The student survival kit has items that could help students get out of a bad situation fast, allow them to defend themselves, and call for help. Some college campuses are considering permitting students to carry a firearm, but it is absolutely essential you check with the school's policies regarding carrying a concealed weapon. Active-shooting scenarios are becoming more and more prevalent, and unfortunately, a school campus is not immune to such assaults. There are also weather situations to contend with. Although rare, they can occur. Parents, teachers, and other caregivers need to consider what items students should have to get them through the chaos until help can get to them.

STUDENT SURVIVAL KIT

The student survival kit can be carried in the student's everyday backpack and/or purse. Most of the gear will be able to fit into a small pack and most students already have a few of the items. Lockers make great caches (secure places to store supplies). If the full kit is too much for your student to carry, have him keep some of the gear in his locker. Many middle school and high school children have lockers, but most elementary students do not. An elementary school survival kit could be sewn into an existing backpack or put into a side or outer pocket. Bottom line, students need to have a means to communicate. They need to know whom to call and basic instructions on what to do. The kit should have some food, water, and a comfort item like a little game, a family picture, or a goal list, something to let them know there is light at the end of the tunnel and to occupy their time in a bad situation.

Pack

The items in this kit are small enough to fit into any standard backpack that your child chooses to carry.

Phone and Emergency Contact List

Phone

A phone is your child's best bet and fastest way to reach out to authorities and get help if she's ever in danger at school. Teach your children how to dial 9-1-1 so the police can get to their location immediately. Younger students may not be able to keep phones with them in class, but it may be possible for them to be kept in a locker. An inexpensive option would be to give younger students a prepaid cell phone with just emergency numbers programmed into the phone. Such a phone would not need to have games, texting, or a camera and its sole purpose would be to serve as your child's emergency communication device.

College students should also have 9-1-1 preprogramed into their phones as well as the phone number to the campus police. They should also keep their phones charged and readily available. This should not be a problem for most college students.

Emergency Contact List

Emergency contacts are important to have programmed into your child's phone. In addition to 9-1-1 and the campus police, important contact information for students of any age includes phone numbers for parents and other guardians and the doctor's office. College students may also want to include phone numbers for their roommate(s), best friend, taxi, and the sober/ safe ride home line. Having these numbers preprogrammed into a cell phone makes them easier to access in an emergency.

Water Bottle

While it's always important to have a way to stay hydrated, a water bottle can also be used for self-defense. Students can throw a bottle to hit and disorient an assailant. If thirty students are cornered, but throw their water bottles at an active shooter, they may be able to injure or disorient the person, perhaps even slow him down and maybe stall the attack.

Granola Bar

A granola bar, energy bar, or nuts can help with energy levels and comfort. If your child might be at school for an extended period of time she will have some food to help her get through the situation.

Emergency Whistle

Every child, teenager, and adult knows how to use a whistle. An emergency whistle can quickly let others know there is a problem and help is needed.

Water Bottle and Snack

Emergency Blanket

If the school loses power, an emergency blanket will help your child stay warm without taking up too much room in the kit. These blankets are also useful if your child or someone else goes into shock.

Comfort Item

A comfort item can help a person of any age stay focused and keep his mind off of the situation at hand. This is especially true for young children. A small toy, game, or a coloring book can help relieve some stress. A goal list and a picture of one's family or loved ones can help maintain focus and determination and keep him saying that he will see his family again. This comfort item can help him cope and get through a stressful situation.

Sweatshirt and Extra Change of Clothes

In case your child has to spend a night at school, make sure he has a sweatshirt and even an extra change of clothes to keep in his locker.

Breath of Life Emergency Escape Mask

See chapter five for more on the description of the Breath of Life Emergency Escape Mask. This is recommended gear for most of the kits in this book. The mask could help a student escape from a burning building or a building with a fuel or chemical leak, and give them time to breathe and get to a safe location.

Pepper Spray

Pepper spray is a must for a college student and can be used to ward off any type of attack, whether it's while walking or in the classroom or dorm. Pepper spray with a 10- to 20-foot (3- to 6-meter) range is ideal because it will allow the student to get behind some type of cover (desk, chair, or behind a corner) before she deploys the spray. Teach your children to hit the

**Pepper Spray
for College
Students**

assailant with the spray then follow up by throwing something fairly heavy to cause injury. Throw books, chairs, or a water bottle to slow down and disorient the attacker and buy time to get away or find a better position to hide until help arrives. It's important to note that most states have age requirements for pepper spray and it is considered assault when it is deployed against someone without provocation. If your child is old enough to carry pepper spray, select one that has a good range and is easy to use. Select a spray that will shoot a long stream at the attacker to provide better distance between the student and the attacker. Avoid fogging and foam pepper sprays for this particular kit.

Forcible Entry Tool
A forcible entry tool is like a multitool on steroids. It looks like a super-strong nail remover but is larger with a sharpened end. It is very durable and can be used to get a college-aged student out of a building or car by helping him open doors, break a lock, smash a window, or pry things open. The tool is a bit heavy but should still be able to fit in a basic backpack. This could prove invaluable to open doors in an active-shooter situation, burning building, or other scenario where he needs to get out quickly.

In light of the active shootings going on in the United States, teachers are being trained about how to deal with and get through an active-shooter scenario, as well as weather scenarios

Forcible Entry Tool

and other disasters. Teachers may want to consider keeping a purse survival kit or an everyday carry kit in their classrooms. Those who prepare can survive. This certainly includes our children's teachers.

SURVIVAL TIP #10: TEACHING CHILDREN AND TEENS TO BE PREPARED

As parents and caregivers, you need to teach your children to be ready and prepared when something bad happens. Turn it into a game at dinner and pose questions about what they would do in given situations. In general, when something bad happens, like an active-shooter situation, teach your children this action plan:

1. **Get out.** Get out of danger and out of the building if possible. Do what you've got to do to get away.
2. **Hide out.** Lock a door, block it, or get behind things that can slow down or stop a bullet like desks, books, chairs, and walls. Silence cell phones and make sure those around you stay quiet as well.
3. **Take action** (this should be for older students and only as a last resort). Throw anything you can get your hands on

in mass assault on the shooter(s) to try to disable him, slow him down, and stop him.

4. **Wait.** When the threat is over, wait for law enforcement to sound the all clear, evacuate, and come out with your hands up in a non-threatening manner.

Like a tornado drill, many schools are rehearsing active-shooter situations. When your child has drills at school, discuss what happened at school that day. Ask her what she did and where she is supposed to go and whom she is supposed to meet up with. Talk with her about what to do if the primary exit is blocked and what other options she might have.

Be sure to also address weather situations and what might happen if the weather is bad and your child has to spend the night at school. As the parent, find out who the point of contact is. Perhaps it's the principal or the teacher. Find out and reinforce this with your child. If your child has a phone and clothes at school, talk through all of these things so he will feel confident about what to do should bad weather strike.

SUMMARY

In a disaster situation, all individuals, including students, need to do their part to stay safe, protect themselves and their fellow students, and do their best to survive. Even young children can and should carry gear that will keep them safe and prepared. Keep the kits age-appropriate and work with your child's school to ensure your child has what he needs to be safe and ready. Teach your children how to use the gear they carry. Make the practice interesting and age-appropriate.

CHAPTER ELEVEN

EXTREME COLD WEATHER KIT

THE SURVIVAL SCENARIO

It's late May in Colorado and you and two friends plan to go hike a "fourteener" [also known as a 14,000-foot (4-kilometer) mountain]. There are many throughout the state and more than a few close to Denver. You and your friends plan to fly into Denver on a Friday night, get up at 4:00 a.m. on Saturday, drive to the closest 14,000-foot (4-meter) mountain, and start your hike before the sun comes up. You and your friends are in decent shape and you feel confident you can hike up the mountain, get some great pictures, and be back in Denver by 8:00 p.m. for dinner. The temperatures have been at least 80°F (27°C) all week in Denver, and though the weather is always a little bit cooler in the mountains, it's nothing you are too concerned about as you know it is always sunny in Colorado.

You arrive in Denver and everything goes as planned: You get in on Friday, get good rest, and have all of your hiking gear packed and ready to go. You are all planning for a spring hike and you are wearing shorts, bringing hydration bladders, a water bottle, a few snacks, phones, a map, a compass, and a light windbreaker. You arrive at the crack of dawn and get moving fast. You check the weather and temperatures for Denver are still the same and farther west in the mountains, the temperatures and conditions look the same as they were prior to your arrival.

You get rolling along your hike and are making great time, however, however, when you approach the summit, things start to get bad. Clouds block out the brilliant sun you had earlier in the morning, the wind is picking up and howling, and temperatures have been plummeting. You reach for your light windbreaker and get it on, but it is hardly doing anything to stop the wind. That is when it starts raining hard. The rain turns to sleet and the three of you are in panic mode. You are maybe thirty minutes from the summit, but it is getting harder and harder to see and the sleet seems to be hitting you from every angle. One of your buddies begins to wander and gets a blank look on his face and starts to shiver. Then the shivering starts for the rest of you. It keeps getting colder and colder and now you are all wet, cold, and the sleet begins to turn to snow and whiteout conditions. All of you are saying this should not be happening: It is almost June and is supposed to be 80°F (27°C) down in Denver! Cold, wet, and freezing, you can't see. What do the three of you do now?

THE ANALYSIS

Always pack for the conditions you are going to be in, expect the worst, and never trust the weather. Research past weather conditions to see if any patterns emerge. Although the hikers in this scenario packed for a normal day, they did not pack for contingencies. Be flexible when things don't go according to your original plan. Be able to rapidly adapt to your given situation. You know you are ready for Mother Nature to throw anything at you. If the weather or terrain presents new and difficult situations, modify your plan, route, and timeline so you can stay safe. In this case, once the weather started to look sketchy, the hikers should have probably turned around and beat feet back to their vehicle as fast as possible.

EXTREME COLD WEATHER KIT GEAR LIST

☐ Pack

☐ Water bottle

☐ Purification tabs and drops

☐ Emergency bivy sack

☐ All-weather extreme sleeping bag

☐ Warming layers

☐ Poncho

☐ Lighter

☐ Stormproof matches

☐ Outdoor stove

☐ Cooking pots and utensils

☐ Candles

☐ Emergency food

☐ Powdered soup (broth, bouillon, etc.)

☐ Phone

☐ Compass

☐ Maps

☐ Whistle

☐ Headlamp

☐ First aid kit

☐ Avalanche beacon

☐ Avalanche vest

☐ Shovel

☐ Knife or multitool

THE TAKEAWAY

Extreme weather can paralyze experienced, seasoned, outdoor enthusiasts in the their tracks. For instance, the 60-mph (96-kpm) winds of New Hampshire's Mount Washington frequently blow unsuspecting hikers off course simply because their instinct is to go with the wind rather than into it. Of course, you don't have to be on a mountain to encounter extremely cold conditions. Just as you wouldn't hike Mount Washington or Mount Hood in shorts and a T-shirt, you want to ensure you have the right kit packed to deal with conditions that can change on a dime.

EXTREME COLD WEATHER KIT

Have the right gear with you and plan for extreme weather that can roll in rapidly and leave you stranded. The gear in this kit will also help prevent hypothermia, a dangerous condition in which a person's core body temperature drops below 95°F (35°C). The cold, wind, and rain can lead to a dangerous situation if you are not prepared for it. These extreme cold weather changes call for an extreme cold weather kit.

Pack

As mentioned before, ensure you get a pack that is right for you. Look for comfort, fit, the capacity to carry the recommended gear list, and any additional items.

Water

Two water bottles need to be a part of your extreme weather kit. Wide-mouth water bottles, like a Nalgene bottle, are a good choice because you can stuff the water bottles with snow. Keep the bottles close to your body and let your body heat melt the snow so it is ready to drink. WARNING: Do this only when you are moving and putting forth effort. Do not attempt to melt snow with your body heat if you are stationary and trying to stay warm, as this will only lower your body temperature.

If you are hunkered down because of the weather, get a fire going and use your stove and cooking gear to melt snow. As the old saying goes, do not pick yellow snow to melt and drink. Remember, there is also mountain runoff, creeks, and streams you can get water from. If you get water from a stream, be sure to use your purification tablets or drops. If you are encountering glacial runoff or ice melts at high altitude, the water should be safe to drink. When in doubt, play it safe and protect yourself by purifying the water.

Shelter

Ensure you have something in your kit to block the wind, snow, hail, and rain. Having layered sheltered protection is the best, especially in extreme conditions. Being inside your bag—which is inside your bivy sack, which is inside your shelter—could allow you to ride out a bad storm for several days. Also keep in mind that the gear you bring can add to or reinforce some form of shelter the environment might give you such as a cave, overhang, or vegetation.

- **Sleeping Bag.** Pack a cold-weather sleeping bag that is rated for the worst conditions you expect. If you think it can get to -20°F (-29°C) or less, make sure you have a bag that is rated for that temperature. Most of these bags have a hood or are designed so you can cocoon up in them by zipping up the bag so your body and head are completely enclosed. With a bivy sack and shelter, you should be able to weather the storm. Many bags come with compression sacks that will shrink down the bag to create more storage room. If yours does not, make sure you get one to maximize the room in your bag. With a sleeping bag in a compression sack, you can save space and have more kit in your pack. Remember the extreme weather bag is going to be denser, and therefore heavier, than your average sleeping bag, but it may

Sleeping Bag

Emergency Bivy

mean the difference between life and death in whiteout conditions and when a wind chill is well below zero. Down bags are more comfortable and warmer, but they are heavier and not meant to get wet. If they do get wet, they become heavy and take a long time to dry. Synthetic bags can be used in wet conditions and still perform. Synthetics are made out of lighter materials and will add less weight to your kit than a down sleeping bag.

- **Bivy Sack.** When dealing with extreme cold, you want to have the Cadillac of bivy sacks, the emergency bivy, which will keep you warm and dry by reflecting most of your body's heat back to you. Put your cold weather sleeping bag inside the emergency bivy and stay warm, dry, and toasty.

- **Tent.** You can also consider packing a one- or two-man tent in your extreme cold weather kit. This is an excellent option, but remember, with more gear comes more weight to shoulder and pack, possibly for days. If you know the conditions are going to be bad, make sure you pack a tent. For example, if you were going to hike Mount Hood, Mount McKinley, Mount Rainier, or Mount Washington, you would definitely want to include a tent in your kit. You more than likely would not be going it alone, so you could spread the gear among your buddies. Remember who has what and make sure you don't get separated or lost.
- **Clothing.** Have appropriate warming layers in the form of polypropylene or silk undergarments. These materials

Sunglasses

Additional Clothing

Cooking
Stove, Pan and
Fire Starter

help keep you warm and wick moisture away from your skin. Wool is a great cold-weather material. It can still keep you warm even if it gets wet. You want to avoid cotton materials and materials that have no wicking action once they get wet.

- **Goggles or Sunglasses.** Sunglasses offer protection from the sun and can serve as safety goggles if needed. At the very least, purchase an inexpensive pair of sunglasses and a neck lanyard so your sunglasses are always handy when you need them.

Fire Starters and Cooking

Have a stormproof lighter, stormproof matches, and a blast match fire starter in your kit. Include some WetFire Tinder Cubes to get a fire going. For extreme weather, you should have some type of stove with you and a cooking container. Select a stove that is lightweight, cooks fast, and has minimal moving parts so it is easy to operate. There are many types of stoves on the market that take many types of fuel—white gas, kerosene, etc. Choose a stove that is easy to operate and one that doesn't require you to pack an inordinate amount of gear for sustained cooking. A white gas stove is a good option. This type of stove has different size fuel bottles that you can attach to the stove.

You can carry one or two fuel bottles, your stove, and food and be able to cook for a few weeks.

Choose cookware that is light, fits into your pack well, and will meet your needs. You could get by on a military canteen cup—although there are lighter pieces of cookware on the market, the canteen cup is a tried and true, battle-tested, almost indestructible piece of gear. You can have a fork/spork combination or utensils made from titanium. The titanium utensils will be more expensive, but they are more durable. Know there are many options when choosing a stove, cookware, and cooking utensils. Find the ones that work best for you, fit into your budget, and can keep the weight of your pack down.

Candles can be used in a shelter to give you light and help increase the temperature by a few degrees. They can be very helpful if you have to hunker down for a day or two because of extreme weather. Make sure you have a hole in your shelter to vent off the carbon monoxide produced by you and the candle.

Emergency Food

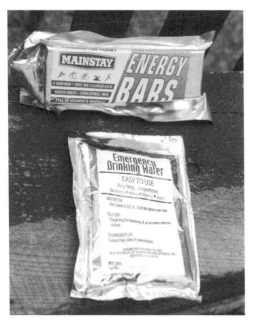

Food

In addition to the emergency food rations that have been discussed in the previous chapters, soup or broth is a good addition to your cold-weather kit. Bouillon cubes or powder are light and compact and are an easy way to warm up your insides and provide some warmth and comfort. For survival in the cold, you are also going to need calorie-rich fat and carbohydrate meals to maintain your energy levels. Granola is a great addition to your extreme weather food kit. It is rich in calories and has good fats. Although there are several types of protein bars on the market that are balanced in carbohydrates, fats, and proteins, be aware that they might freeze and not be palatable when you need to eat them. Find foods that are easy to prepare, easy to snack on, and nutrient rich to put in your extreme weather kit.

Store your food in resealable plastic bags, which are easy to organize and label. You can also pack MREs or freeze-dried foods that you can rehydrate. Rehydration should not be too big of an issue as long as you have a reliable stove and snow you can melt to prepare your freeze-dried food.

Security and Communication

Make sure you have the following security and communication items in your extreme-cold kit: cell phone, compass, maps, whistle, a multitool or Swiss Army knife, headlamp, and first aid kit. You'll also want to include a two-way radio in your kit so you can communicate to a base camp, the ranger station, and emergency agencies in case you get in trouble. Pack extra batteries for your radio and cell phone. Establish check-in windows with these groups to give them updates and status reports. Have contingency plans in place if you miss communication check-in windows and decide in advance if you will return to your last known position or even abort your camping/hiking expedition. Make sure you've discussed these things with everyone in your party before your departure.

If you know you are going to be in an avalanche-prone area, an avalanche beacon, vest, and shovel are a must. An avalanche beacon sends out a signal on a certain frequency so buried avalanche victims can be located. Everyone in your party should be wearing an avalanche beacon, including yourself. An avalanche vest is another piece of equipment to consider including in your kit. If you are buried in an avalanche, the vest lets you breathe for a longer period while under the snow. A shovel will help you dig out snow to create a cave to sleep in. It can also help you dig out others who may have been buried in an avalanche.

SURVIVAL TIP # 11: SURVIVING THE COLD AT NIGHT

If you find yourself in a survival situation in an extremely cold environment, make sure you eat fats in the evening before you go to sleep to help you stay warm at night. Your body will burn the fat throughout the night and in turn help keep you warm. Eat carbs during the day to maintain your energy levels.

Dig a cold hole (or sleep shelf) or make a snow cave for sleeping. Use a shovel to dig a long, rectangular hole that is lower than where you are sleeping. Cold air will move into the hole and keep you slightly warmer in your higher position. If you decide to construct a cave, you want to do the same thing which is to sleep on a shelf inside the cave. If you are going to attempt

A NOTE ON MOVING IN EXTREME COLD

Try to move and work with the least amount of clothing or layers on as possible and don't completely overexert yourself. Why? You don't want to start to sweat and get what you are wearing wet. If you get wet, make sure you have another shirt you can change into when you stop or bed down. As it has been said before, you don't want to be cold and wet. Being wet in extremely cold conditions can quickly cause hypothermia.

to sleep inside a cave, look at where you are and see if you can take advantage of anything like an overhang, built-up snow, or a snow bank you could dig into. Make sure you pack the snow down and make it as compact as possible. Then dig a trench or tunnel into the compacted snow and carve out an internal space. Try to do this where you would be protected from any falling debris or an avalanche. You don't want to get swept away if you can use a rock outcropping or a group of trees to protect you. Dig out the internal space and construct a shelf to sleep on. You can poke a small hole through the roof of your cave for carbon dioxide to escape. Use your pack to block the entrance to your cave to keep some of the heat in. Also make a shelf so you can burn a candle in your sleep shelter/cave. A candle will raise the temperature inside, but remember to have a hole so the carbon dioxide can vent out of your cave. Don't make your cave/shelter so large that you have so much space you are no longer insulating yourself with the snow. You should be able to move around inside and it should be able to accommodate you and your gear comfortably. Anything you can do to help you stay warm can and should be done in an extreme cold weather environment.

SUMMARY

Get a good, comfortable pack that can fit all of your extreme cold weather gear and practice with your kit. Hike with your extreme cold weather kit in the spring and summer so you get used to the load. Practice using the kit that is filled with the recommended gear from the list and the gear that you come up with on your own so you are more proficient with all of the items. Develop the muscle memory that will allow you to efficiently access and use the items in your kit so when you are in a cold weather environment you can stay warm, use the tools you have, and get back home safely.

CHAPTER TWELVE

MARITIME SURVIVAL KIT

THE SURVIVAL SCENARIO

Your dive boat breaks down on a trip to the island of Cozumel, Mexico. You are out at sea and cannot see any land. The boat is dead in the water, there's a short in the boat's communication system, and cell phones aren't getting any coverage. In short, nothing is working. You start to drift and the seas begin to get rougher. The wind picks up. The sky turns dark, the waves get bigger, and the dive boat is still dead in the water. Large swells begin hitting the craft and the boat begins to take on water. The stern begins to tip and you don't know how much longer you are going to be able to stay on the boat before it sinks. You know you have your buoyancy compensator device to keep you afloat and you have a wet suit. You know the other divers have this gear as well. You all have compasses on your dive gauges, so you could swim if you had to. It looks like the crew has been bailing out the water at the back of the boat and the boat is stable, but you are still dead in the water. What do you do next?

THE ANALYSIS

This is not a situation any of us want to be in. This actually happened and the boat ended up sinking and thousands of dollars

MARITIME SURVIVAL KIT GEAR LIST

- ☐ Pack
- ☐ Waterproof compression sack
- ☐ Plastic food storage bags, various sizes
- ☐ Survival knife
- ☐ Multitool
- ☐ Breath of Life Emergency Escape Mask
- ☐ Gear Aid Explorer Field Repair Kit
- ☐ Duct tape
- ☐ Aurora Fire Starter (silver)
- ☐ UCO Stormproof Match Kit (25 matches/green) x 2
- ☐ WetFire Tinder Cubes (pack of 8)
- ☐ Standard Emergency Survival Fishing Kit x 2
- ☐ Emmrod Pack-Rod casting fishing pole
- ☐ MSR XGK Stove Combo
- ☐ MSR Quick 2 Cooking System
- ☐ MSR Titan Fork and Spoon
- ☐ Global compass
- ☐ Headlamp
- ☐ Midland XT511 Base Camp Radio (hand-crank)
- ☐ Survival mirror
- ☐ JetScream survival whistle
- ☐ MSR Sweetwater Microfilter

worth of dive gear was lost to the sea, but luckily everyone made it back to shore. The boat was close enough to shore that the crew and divers could swim in.

- [ ] Nalgene Silo (white) 48 oz (1 L) x 2
- [ ] Aquamira Water Treatment Drops
- [ ] Platypus Big Zip LP 2L (68 oz) water bladder
- [ ] Handheld desalination unit (pricey, but worth it in a crunch)
- [ ] Wiggy's Super Light sleeping bag
- [ ] Wiggy's Bivy Sack (waterproof, multicam)
- [ ] MSR MarPad-Lite sleeping pad
- [ ] Rain poncho (green)
- [ ] Bathing wipes
- [ ] Insect repellent
- [ ] Bug head net
- [ ] Freeze-dried food pack (5 each)
- [ ] Emergency 1,200-calorie food bar (5 each)
- [ ] Emergency drinking water packs (10 each)
- [ ] UDAP Bear Spray #12
- [ ] Monkey fist
- [ ] Emergency beacon
- [ ] Flare gun with flares
- [ ] Marine 200 Medical Kit (Includes emergency medical guide)
- [ ] *SAS Survival Handbook*
- [ ] *Sea Survival Handbook*

THE TAKEAWAY

Think about being out on your own boat, either in the lake or ocean. What gear and supplies should you have in your maritime survival kit? It is now time to think amphibious and use your survival skills and knowledge of the sea to put together your maritime survival kit.

MARITIME SURVIVAL KIT

This kit has everything you need for a maritime environment with all the components of survival covered—water, food, fire, shelter, and security. Equally important are the backup items that build redundancy into the kit. When it comes to preparing for the worst, one is none and two is a good place to start. The maritime kit starts with a strong, durable waterproof bag and individually waterproofed pieces of gear that include fire starters, cooking kit, food, water, signaling devices, repair kits, food gathering devices, and more.

This is gear that has been tested by the experts and put through the ringer for performance and reliability.

The Pack

When choosing a pack for an aquatic environment, the SealLine Pro Pack is the most durable and waterproof option. This pack is used by the military when they operate in and around the water. This pack will keep your gear dry, secure, and easy to access.

Dry Bag

Field Repair Kit

Make sure you take extra steps to waterproof your gear. Place the smaller items in this kit in plastic food storage bags. Place the gear in the bags, remove the air from the bags, and then place the bags into a trash bag. Gooseneck the trash bag with a rubber band. After you remove the air from the trash bag, place it in a waterproof compression sack and cinch it down tight. Place the compression sack in your pack. The SealLine Pro Pack will be able to hold all of the recommended items for the maritime survival kit.

Survival Tools

A reliable knife, multitool, duct tape, and Breath of Life Emergency Escape Mask should be part of your maritime survival kit. Another item that you should have in this kit is something to repair your kit, such as the Gear Aid Explorer Field Repair Kit. This is a small kit that allows you to fix or modify items in the maritime kit while you're out in the field.

FIRE STARTERS

As you would probably expect, stormproof matches and Wet-Fire Tinder Cubes are essential parts of the maritime kit. These will help you get a fire started and keep it burning. Another

Cooking Gear

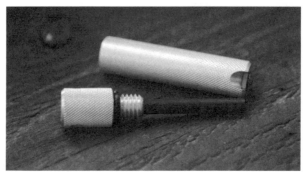

Aurora Fire
Starter

option for getting a fire started is the Aurora Fire Starter, which
has been approved by the Navy Diver Challenge in addition to
being recommended by the authors. This fire starter has been
put to the test in every climate and place, but especially in and
around an aquatic environment. This starter creates sparks to
light your kindling and get a fire going in addition to having
hardened steel on the back of the device that will allow you to
sharpen your knife.

Food Gathering

For food gathering you will want to have two standard fishing
kits. Fishing kits consist of fishing line, bobbers, lead weights,
and hooks. For each kit, you should have two rolls of fishing
line, at least three bobbers, at least five lead weights, and ten

Emmrod Pack-Rod Pole and Survival Fishing Kit

hooks in varying sizes. Remember, redundancy is a must, especially when it comes to making sure you have enough to eat.

Include an Emmrod Pack-Rod casting fishing pole, which is a small, compact fishing pole that breaks down and easily fits in your pack.

Cooking

Consider that you might need to cook while on your boat, craft, and/or land when you run into it. A stove kit that includes a fuel source, pots, and pans in addition to the stove is a good option. If you are concerned about weight, select a kit with a limited amount of pots and pans.

MSR Titan Fork and Spoon

The Titan Fork and Spoon are made of titanium so they are ultra light and super strong. They will not break on you and can be used repeatedly.

Compass, Radio, Mirror, and Whistle

Navigation and Communication

Include a good compass in your maritime survival kit, but also include at least one other backup, such as a wrist compass, Silva Ranger compass, or global compass.

A signal mirror, survival whistle, hand-crank radio, and headlamp are all items you'll want to pack in your maritime survival kit. When packing, store the headlamp and the radio each in its own waterproof container. As discussed earlier, a waterproof container is simply a ziplock bag or two with your kit inside. Make sure the air is out and the bag is sealed. For electronic gear, we like to use multiple ziplock bags to make sure it remains dry. When you need your electronic items, headlamp, or radio take them out of your bag, remove them from their individual waterproof containers, use them, then re-waterproof them again and stow them away in your waterproof bag. Don't leave them out in the open where they can get wet or fall overboard. Use the gear you need and when done, stow it away and keep it secure.

Remember, a flash from your signal mirror can be seen for miles and miles on the water, so pack one or two in your kit.

Have an emergency beacon in your kit as well. This beacon has been discussed earlier in the book. We recommend sacrificing a few luxuries or meals eaten at a restaurant to save up and get one of these. This is a mission-essential piece of gear if you know you are going to be out at sea.

Water

Have multiple options for securing safe drinking water. Bags, bladders, tarps, poncho, raincoat, water bottles, pots, and pans can all be used to capture rainwater, which can be consumed without any filter. If you do collect water you want to be able to store it. A bladder, water bottles, plastic bags, and food storage bags can be used to capture and store water. If all of your gear is individually waterproofed in your large dry bag, you could potentially remove it and use your dry bag as a large water-capturing device. This could be an option on a beach, land, or while at sea if you get a lot of rain. If you hit land or an island, you should also have a water filter that can filter out pathogens. You can't filter out salt in water, so don't try to use your filter while out at sea.

Another option is to include a handheld desalination unit. These units are very costly, but it could mean the difference between life and death if saltwater is your only option for water

MSR Sweet-
Water Filter
and Water
Bottle

Sleeping
Bag, Pad, and
Poncho

and is definitely a consideration when you are putting together
your maritime survival kit.

Shelter

Be aware of the type of temperature and environment you might
encounter and pack the necessary shelter, including:

- **Sleeping Bag.** Even during the summer, the night gets cool.
  A light sleeping bag, such as Wiggy's Super Light sleeping bag, will keep you warm and cozy at night out at sea.
  The temperature rating for this bag is 0°F (-18°C). If you
  are concerned about the weather getting especially cold,
  pack a heavier sleeping bag in the kit.
- **Bivy Sack.** A bivy sack does not take up much space in
  your kit and will only add to your warmth at night. Wiggy's Bivy Sack is a great option.
- **Sleeping Pad.** A sleeping pad can keep you more comfortable and help keep some insulation between you
  and the boat and sea. It makes for more comfortable,
  restful sleep.
- **Rain Poncho.** This is a standard poncho to help keep you
  dry on the deck in adverse weather conditions. You could
  also make the poncho into a shelter from the sun and use
  it as a catch to direct and gather water.

Personal Hygiene

Bathing wipes can help with personal hygiene and make you feel as if you took a shower when you are not near one. They can also take off the salt and grime from being out at sea.

You will encounter flies and other bugs while out at sea. If you are trying to get a good night of sleep a bug head net will be handy, even out in the open ocean. Also include insect repellant such as Ben's 100 Max Spray Pump, which has the maximum amount of DEET in the formula.

Food and Water

Make sure you have an ample supply of food and water that can last for days. Put what you can fit in your pack, especially water. Load as much water as possible. As a minimum, include five packs of freeze-dried food, five emergency 1,200-calorie food bars, and ten emergency drinking water packs.

Personal Protection

Include bear spray in your kit in case you have to ward off marauders and/or incapacitate an unruly member of your party. Hit the target hard with the spray and get it under control. If you need to repel someone trying to board your ship, blast him with as much spray as possible. A monkey fist can be used as a weapon in close quarters, or you can also use it for what it is truly designed for: a weight at the end of a line that you throw. In a maritime environment, you can attach your monkey fist to the end of 550 paracord to throw it to another craft or a pier to link up with a friendly party or help anchor you to a fixed structure or land.

Use your flare gun to signal for help or you could use it as a weapon in case someone is trying to get on your craft.

Medical Kit and References

Add the Marine 200 Medical Kit, which includes an emergency medical guide, as well as the *SAS Survival Handbook* and the

Sea Survival Handbook to your maritime survival kit. The Marine 200 Medical Kit will help with first aid, while the *SAS Survival Handbook* is a great survival resource for any situation. The *Sea Survival Handbook* is another valuable tool to have in your kit because it specifically addresses being stranded at sea.

SURVIVAL TIP #12: LEARN HOW TO SWIM

If you don't know how to swim, take a swim course from the American Red Cross or SwimAmerica. These courses are offered all around the United States. Don't be ashamed if you don't know how to swim as an adult—swallow your pride and take a class or learn from a swim coach. Learn from a certified coach so you can learn the proper techniques from the start. In any of these courses you will learn basic survival techniques including how to: relax, slow your breathing, preserve your energy, float, and even rescue yourself. If you make the claim of being a survivalist or someone who is prepared, you need to be confident in an aquatic environment. Learning how to swim and knowing some basic water survival skills could save your life.

SUMMARY

Prepare for the worst at sea. If you know you are going to be on a ship, seagoing vessel, or even on what you think is a routine boat dive trip, bring your maritime survival kit with you. If you pack what is recommended in this kit, you should be able to sustain yourself almost indefinitely if you get lost at sea. If you end up hitting land, you will be ready to set up camp and continue to survive until help arrives.

CHAPTER THIRTEEN

ULTIMATE BUG OUT KIT

THE SURVIVAL SITUATION

Almost everyone has an emergency story. It may be a weather-related event, police action, military action, or some type of mechanical failure such as a car breaking down. Joel's story happened on September 11, 2001, and he recounts it here: At the time I was living in Arlington, Virginia, just a few miles from the Pentagon. The day started out like most other days. I was working in Ashburn, Virginia, which was a 45-minute drive away from the house I shared with three roommates in Arlington. After the Pentagon was attacked, most people in my office decided it was best to head for the door and make their way home. I was no different and made my way back home by about noon.

The few hours after the second tower fell are blurry to me. One of my roommates got home at some point and said that he had heard car bombs were going off in Washington, D.C., and a lot of people were dead. The fog of war had settled in my mind. I can't remember if we ever made contact with my other roommates because cell service was spotty. At some point my roommate who was home, Mark, and I decided the best move would be to bug out to West Virginia where his parents owned a home. My roommate was shocked when I came downstairs in my full

ULTIMATE BUG OUT KIT GEAR LIST

- ☐ Pack
- ☐ Shelf-stable water
- ☐ Water filtering system, purification tables
- ☐ Water bladder or plastic or aluminum bottles
- ☐ Freeze-dried food or MREs
- ☐ Edible plant guide
- ☐ Shelf-stable energy bars
- ☐ Stormproof matches, ferrocerium rod, cigarette lighter, and/or magnifying glass
- ☐ WetFire Tinder Cubes or steel wool
- ☐ Stove or camping grill
- ☐ Pots and silverware
- ☐ Slingshot
- ☐ Snares
- ☐ Packable fishing pole, lures, and fishing line
- ☐ .22 rifle or pellet gun with ammunition
- ☐ Multitool
- ☐ 550 paracord
- ☐ Bivy sack or tarp

Marine Corps camouflage uniform with what I thought at the time was an ultimate bug out bag, which was really just a mismatch of old military gear. I remember my roommate looking at me and saying, "What are you doing?" I told him that I had put the uniform on in case we hit roadblocks; I might be able to

- ☐ Three- or four-season tent
- ☐ Sleeping bag
- ☐ Sleeping pad
- ☐ Additional clothing
- ☐ Bear spray
- ☐ Night vision goggles
- ☐ Scoped rifle
- ☐ Flashlight
- ☐ Radio
- ☐ Compass
- ☐ GPS
- ☐ Personal Hygiene and First Aid Kits
- ☐ Dental
- ☐ Toilet paper or bathing wipes
- ☐ Basic first aid kit with some advance capability
- ☐ Local currency (small bills)
- ☐ Gold and silver coins
- ☐ Cigarettes and alcohol
- ☐ Bug Out Vehicle

get us through with the uniform on. I know it was a stretch but we didn't have accurate information on what was going on in the country and anything seemed possible. So with bag in hand, what little food we could grab, and a 9mm pistol, we headed to West Virginia.

THE ANALYSIS

The point of this story is that Joel was totally unprepared for the situation. Yes, he had a backpack with some MREs and limited gear. Yes, he had a 9mm pistol with maybe two boxes of ammo (one hundred rounds) and whatever food was in the refrigerator. Beyond that, he had nothing. If it would have been a real situation, he would have been a victim of the situation, not a survivor.

After that experience, we immediately started brainstorming on what anyone would need in an emergency bag. How long would it sustain a person? Would it provide food? Would it allow someone to get more food? How would you purify water? What would be the perfect shelter?

Joel's emergency situation was due to an attack on the United States but no matter where you live, you must be prepared. The coastlines are vulnerable to hurricanes and typhoons. Inland locations are prone to severe weather and earthquakes. Countries around the world, including the United States, are susceptible to currency devaluation, riots, and civil unrest. The unprepared will grow desperate in these situations and you must be prepared to move out of the affected area or live off the land.

THE TAKEAWAY

The bug out bag provides the type of insurance money can't buy. When things go bad and your credit cards and cash will not work, our society, which relies on the 24-hour availability of food, will get ugly fast. There is a saying among survivalists that America is eight meals away from anarchy. Meaning that if people miss more than eight meals in a row (2½ days) things will go south in a hurry and desperate people will do things that no one thought was possible. People will steal and kill for food and clean water. And those who are not able to kill or unwilling to kill will be subject to those who are.

THE ULTIMATE BUG OUT KIT

It's worth repeating that what is in your head is the most important survival gear you can carry. When thinking about the gear to go into your ultimate bug out bag, make sure you select items you are comfortable using. Build your bag with gear that will work for you and gear that you know how to use. You don't want the first time you use the gear in your bug out bag to be during a true survival situation.

Pack

Your pack should be sturdy and durable such as a tactical pack, camping pack, or surplus military pack. For tactical packs, Granite Gear, Mystery Ranch, and Eberlestock are reputable brands. For camping packs, consider REI, The North Face, MSR, Lowepro, Kelty, or Arc'teryx; however, most of the brands you'll find at quality camping stores will be made to high standards and be suitable for your ultimate bug out bag. Avoid buying packs at a discount chain store unless you cannot afford anything else. If that is the case, closely examine the stitching

Bug Out Bag

and material of the pack. Look for double- or triple-stitching in critical stress areas like the shoulder.

As you fill your pack, remember that ounces equal pounds and pounds equal pain. The more you put in the pack, the more you will have to carry. Create a "drop list" of items that are luxuries (i.e., extra shoes, winter coat, snow pants, and miscellaneous gear such as shovels) that you can drop along the way if needed. You should never drop the basics of survival: shelter, fire, water containers and water purification, and food or food-procuring items.

You should design your pack for not only the area you live in but also the area you might have to move to in a survival situation. If you plan to head to a colder, less populated location, your bag should reflect that with cold-weather clothes and survival items for cooler weather. The same is true if you plan to head to a warm climate. Your pack should contain clothes that can deal with the worst weather Mother Nature can throw at you. If you live in south Florida, that might be extensive rain gear. Imagine being outside for 24 hours in the worst weather for your climate. That should be how you plan for the clothes that go into your ultimate bug out bag.

Water

Plan to purify and store water. Water weighs a lot so it might not be practical to store water in your bag prior to an emergency. If you really want to pack some extra water, consider shelf-stable water made by Survivor Industries, but also include water purification methods such as a filter system, purification tablets, or the means to boil water. You will also need bottles and bladders to store water. Much consideration should be given to water because you won't last long without it, and drinking bad water can be a fatal mistake that might impair you during a critical time.

Food and Fire

People think they will be able to hunt for food in an emergency. The truth is most people are not good hunters or fishermen, and the amount of calories you get from the food you hunt won't sustain you for long. If you have to err on the side of having too much of one thing, make it food. Food is the Achilles heel of most bug out bags. Pack long-lasting, shelf-stable food such as freeze-dried foods or Meals Ready to Eat (MRE). The downside of freeze-dried food is that you usually have to cook or prepare it with water. The upside of freeze-dried food is that it has a long shelf life (up to twenty years in some cases) and it is light to carry around. The downside to MREs is they only last for three to four years, but the upside is they are ready to eat with little preparation. Either choice will have a much longer shelf life than anything you would find at the grocery store. Also, it's best plan a three- to four-year rotation system for your food so you don't get caught with spoiled food when you need it. You will also need some type of pot or pan that you can use with an open flame but that is still light enough to pack and carry.

Freeze Dried Food Pack

In the event that you will be on your own for an extended period of time, you need to think of ways to catch or hunt food with the items in your bag. Pack a guide to edible plants for finding wild plants you can safely eat. You may also want to pack a slingshot and snares for hunting and a collapsible fishing pole and fishing lures for fishing. You also might consider investing in a low-cost .22 rifle or pellet gun to be stored with your bug out bag. These are great for small game and you can carry a lot of rounds or pellets with very little weight and fairly low cost. Carry at least five hundred rounds of .22LR ammunition, though if you can manage to carry more it would be advisable.

Being able to start a fire is a key element of survival. As we have covered in earlier chapters, you need to have multiple ways to start a fire. Remember: Two is one and one is none. You need at least two ways to start a fire and it is best to have even more options. Stormproof matches, a ferrocerium rod, a cigarette lighter or magnifying glass can work. Also pack several different types of tinder such as steel wool or WetFire Tinder Cubes. While on the go, have a way

BUG OUT BAG TOOL KIT

- ☐ Screwdrivers (both Phillips and standard)
- ☐ Crowbar
- ☐ Allen wrench/hex key set
- ☐ Wire cutters
- ☐ Standard wrench
- ☐ Socket wrench (small set)
- ☐ Full-tang survival knife
- ☐ Gas siphon

YURIY KULIK / SHUTTERSTOCK.COM

Three-Season
Tent

to pick up dry sticks and twigs. Bad weather can hit at any time and you might regret not carrying extra dry tinder.

Tools

You never know when you might need to fix one of the items in your bug out bag, so make sure you have a few tools in your pack. Of course you would like to have every tool with you, but that is not realistic, so stick to the basics and plan out scenarios where you might need certain tools. A nice Leatherman or Gerber multitool will provide you with a lot of the tool options mentioned above as well as a few extra.

Shelter

Shelter is usually down the list of major concerns for an ultimate bug out bag, but it should be right at the top. Being able to get good rest while staying dry and warm should be a top priority when you plan your bag's contents. If you want to go fast and light without a tent, make sure you practice building shelters prior to an emergency. You also might consider having at least one or two tools for shelter building like 550 paracord or a tarp or a bivy sack. If you prefer the comforts of a tent, look for something designed for at least three seasons and back-country camping. These tents usually have the lightest poles and the simplest design. Another consideration for shelter includes how many people you will have to shelter in an emergency. If you have a family of five, you obviously need more than a one-man tent in your bag. Although they add considerable extra weight, you may want to have a sleeping bag and a sleeping pad in your ultimate bug out bag; some good brands to look at are Wiggy's and Therm-a-Rest. You can also pick up used military bags online or at a local surplus store. With a tent, sleeping bag, and sleeping pad, you will not have to compromise on shelter choices. Meaning that if you had to choose between venturing into an abandoned house in the middle of the night or staying in the tree line along a cornfield, you could be in the tree line and be completely comfortable. These are the types of questions you have to ask yourself when determining what goes in your bag.

Security

Carry items that can alert you to a threat or that can create distance between you and a potential threat. Flashlights, night-vision goggles, and binoculars can be used to discover potential threats. Items such as bear spray or firearms can create space between you and a threat.

.45 ACP Rifle

SAMPLE NO-COMMUNICATION PLAN

A no-communication plan might look something like this:

If something major happens and you cannot reach me and I cannot reach you, gather children and discussed items and move to point A1. Try to stay with the children at point A1 as long as possible, if you cannot stay at point A1 or reach point A1, then move to point B1. I will come to point A1 first. If you are not there I will move to point B1 and wait for you there. Please leave notes at each location telling me where you have moved to, along with time and date.

ULTIMATE BUG OUT KIT

Communication and Navigation

For thirty-five dollars you can invest in a rugged mountaineering compass. Get two if you can afford it. You should also have both road maps and topographical maps of the area you live in and the area where you plan to bug out. Plan for mobile phones not to work in a major emergency. However, there have been reports that text messages worked during the aftermath of Hurricane Katrina, so make sure you have the ability to text on your phone. Develop a no-communication plan, which will allow you and your loved ones to eventually meet up at the bug out location.

Personal Hygiene and First Aid

Personal hygiene and medical items are other considerations for your bag. If you don't like wiping with leaves, you better pack some toilet paper. Women need to take considerations if they are on their menstrual cycle. People taking certain required medications need to consider them in their bag planning. Dental, bathing, grooming, and overall wellness are all considerations for your bag. Minor scrapes and cuts, if left untreated, can turn into infected messes. Being able to deal with these issues in the field is a plus. Although we don't recommend overloading on medical items, small kits that can deal with limited trauma are a good idea. If you are a group or a family, you can have small kits for everyone and then have one person who carries the large trauma kit. You can go overboard with medical kits with items for childbirth or major surgery. In the end, what you put in your ultimate bug out bag is up to you, but sticking to the basics for your bag and keeping the other major items in a separate suit-case or kit that can travel with you in your bug out vehicle is a good idea. Remember, there may be a moment when you can't take everything with you, so make sure the stuff you have in your bag covers the essentials.

Money and Bartering Items

During a bug out situation, you might encounter people who have things you need and who might be willing to part with those items for a price. We will never know what items will hold value in a future disaster but if the past holds any lessons, gold has always held some type of value. We recommend you have a mix of local currency (five hundred dollars in small bills, for example), gold coins, silver coins, and barter items such as ciga-rettes, .22LR ammunition, and alcohol.

Bug Out Vehicle

GABRIELA INSURATELU / SHUTTERSTOCK.COM

Bug Out Vehicle

Your method of travel during a time of crisis is something to which you should give great thought. Whether you plan to travel by vehicle, motorcycle, ATV, boat, bicycle, or an animal such as a horse, you have to give extra consideration to not only your method of travel but also the area you plan to travel in and what that area will look like during a crisis.

Freeways and interstates might be clogged during a time of crisis and your best-laid plans might be useless. Your travel plans should have a primary and a secondary option. Depending on your mode of transportation, you need to plan for things like extra gas, spare tires, walking shoes, and vehicle-type tools. You might also store things in your bug out vehicle such as food, water, and shelter. We like to think of our bug out vehicles with an expeditionary mind set. A lot of things you might store in your bug out vehicle will be things you might not necessarily be able to carry with you if you leave the vehicle behind but would be great items to have if you are able to stay close to the vehicle. These items might include heavy-duty shelter, food, water, sleeping bags, camping gear, and weapons. Consult your local laws before you store weapons in your car.

SURVIVAL TIP #13: ALWAYS BE PREPARED

- Your bug out bag should always be packed and ready to go; just insert the things you don't normally store in a bag (food, water, guns, and ammunition)
- Identify locations along your bug out route that sell food and water. They may be your last chance to load up on your way out of town during an emergency.
- Plan a bag bug out bag for each person in your family.

SUMMARY

As you can see from this chapter, you can really "what if" the ultimate bug out bag to death. If you are overwhelmed, a good place to start is to keep a list of everything you do for three days, including eating and drinking. After the three days, go through the list and think about how you would feel if you didn't have that item or activity. If it is a problem, you probably need to add that item to your ultimate bug out bag list. Some people like to read a fiction or religious book every day. Those people should plan to have a book in their bag to help keep them calm during troubling times. Perhaps you like to be able to brush your teeth every day. Then pack at least two toothbrushes and two large tubes of toothpaste in your bag, along with some floss. These items will make you happy and will help you get through a survival situation.

In addition to the three-day list, we also recommend you take a multi-day backcountry camping trip. Make sure you bring a notepad and pen. Take notes on what you like and don't like, what you could use more of, and what you are missing. This is a great exercise to really test your bag and your gear. You can't make your bag better if you don't test it and critique it. If you can afford to do this at least once a year you will be much better prepared when things go south.

If you don't remember anything else from this chapter on ultimate bug out bags, remember this: Stick to the basics. They will get you through any emergency.

CHAPTER FOURTEEN

GET TO KNOW THE AUTHORS

ABOUT MARK PUHALY

Mark graduated from Texas A&M University with a bachelor's of science in biochemistry and completed graduate work in international commerce and policy at George Mason University. Mark is a former Marine Recon Team Leader, Marine Officer Instructor at The Basic School and Marine Infantry Officer. He is an outdoor adventurist and survivalist. Mark has lived and traveled all over the world with the United States Marine Corps.

Mark has raced multiple marathons and competed in numerous triathlons from Sprint to Ironman distance. Mark coaches triathletes, swimmers, and crossfit athletes. When Mark is not working or coaching he is preparing for his next race, spending time with his family, writing articles and thinking about the survival books and topics he wants to write about. Mark has his Crossfit Endurance, Level 1 and Crossfit Mobility Certifications. Mark is also a USA Triathlon Level I coach. Mark makes his home in Texas and is a contributing author to SurvivalCache.com, SHTFBlog.com, and TheSurvivalistBlog.com. Mark also consults with Forge Survival Supply on new gear and private customer engagements.

Q&A WITH MARK PUHALY

How long have you been thinking about and preparing for survival?

Growing up, I was very influenced by my father, who was a Marine and is still the most diligent man I know. I would tag along with him to the gym, for a run, or join a weight workout with him and his veteran buddies in our basement when he was not forcing me to study and do my homework.

Please describe your everyday carry items.

A Glock 30 with two full magazines, Cold Steel Recon 1, Leatherman, iPhone, and Ironman Watch. I also keep a car survival kit in my vehicle. At a minimum, this kit includes water, water purification tabs, food, a space blanket, tools, flares, iPhone car charger, flashlight, compass, firestarter, oil, spare gas, and Kimber Custom pistol. For longer trips, I add more chow and water and I put in clothing that's appropriate for the season and environment I am traveling in or to.

**Mark During the
2012 Ironman in Texas**

What is your favorite bug out pistol?

A Glock 21, large caliber. It has a tremendous Taylor K.O. potential when paired with a .45 round, large capacity magazine. I will take a .45 every day of the week!

Favorite concealed carry pistol?

My trusted Glock 30. Just like the Glock 21 it's a good size and has good stopping power with a large capacity magazine for a .45 round.

Favorite bug out rifle or carbine?

I have a few: FN SCAR-H (.308) or a SOCOM-16. I am lucky enough to have both; there's nothing like a little redundancy with more knockout potential than a .223 round.

What about shotguns? What do you prefer?

My Benelli M-4 Combat Shotgun. It is the shotgun of choice for the United States Marine Corps and it definitely works for me. I like it with a big 12-gauge round on a semi-automatic platform.

How much bug-in food do you keep at your house? At your bug out location?

Six months at home and two years' worth at my bug out location.

Mark (Second from Left) During Filming for Apocalypse 101

Name the most important items in your bug out bag.

- **Water.** I store 20 packets of emergency water and water purification in the form of drops, a water purification straw, water bottle with a built-in filter, and an extra Nalgene bottle.
- **Navigation.** I use a compass, protractor, and map of the area.
- **Signaling items.** Headlamps, Surefire Light, air panel, and strobe are a must.
- **Shelter.** I prefer an emergency bivy sack and 550 paracord.
- **Fire.** I like to use an Aurora fire starter, matches, magnesium block, cotton balls dipped in petroleum jelly, and two lighters.
- **Food.** I pack six days of emergency food.
- **Communication.** I include an iPhone, emergency hand-crank radio, two-way radio, and possibly a beacon depending on the environment I am in.
- **Security.** I have either my M4 carbine rifle or my SOCOM 16 rifle and my custom Kimber as my sidearm.

These are the basics. For a cold-weather environment I pack more gear, including warming layers, a sleeping bag, possibly a tent, stove, and cooking gear.

Describe your bug out location.

It's in the southwest Texas hill country and is an off-grid cabin that is constantly being fortified, improved, and augmented with more gear, food, and water.

Describe your bug out vehicle.

My truck and a mountain bike on the rack loaded with panniers ready for use.

What is your ideal bug out bag?

It might be old school, but I prefer an ALICE military pack. ALICE stands for all-purpose lightweight individual carrying equipment.

Favorite home-defense pistol?

My custom Kimber with Tritium sights and a laser/light combo.

Favorite survival book?

This book, of course!

Favorite survival-type movie?

Army of Darkness (It's a trick, get an ax!).

Favorite survival knife?

Parry blade survival knife.

Survival tools in your kit?

Leatherman.

Have you ever found yourself in a survival situation? What happened, what were the circumstances, and what did you do to get out of it?

I have been lucky enough to get out of a few situations that could have easily turned south rather quickly. Being a Marine and priding myself on being amphibious like all Marines, one story comes to mind. This story involves water, big waves, swells, surge, boats breaking down, getting shocked, and thinking about wanting to swim for the coast while being seven miles (11.2 km) out to sea. This was a large training exercise with Reconnaissance Marines and the US Navy. We were training down in the Florida Keys and this was part of normal training scenarios Recon Marines go through.

The Amphibious Operation from Hell

Our mission was to conduct a confirmatory beach reconnaissance, which is a report used by the military prior to landing on and/or securing a beachhead. The goal is to make sure the beach is safe and can accommodate a larger amphibious landing force, such as small rubber boats (zodiacs), rigid raiding craft (19-foot

[6m] Boston whalers) and amphibious assault vehicles (armored vehicles) and landing craft air cushions (LCACs), which are large hovercraft-type vehicles that can bring in tanks and other motorized equipment.

The mission called for us to insert via a zodiac boat, which is a small rigid inflatable boat, from a larger Patrol, Hydrofoil, Missile (PHM) boat stationed 10 miles 16 (km) from the coast. Our plan was to navigate over the horizon to the target beach, conduct a confirmatory beach reconnaissance, and launch back out to sea, navigating back to the PHM for extract. A confirmatory beach report confirms that the tentative beach for landing is still a viable option. The report includes a survey of the beach, the hinterland, egress routes, a surf report, beach gradient, and beach composition.

The weather conditions were bad at sea during the insert. Swells reached 6–12 feet (2–4m) and got worse during the mission and continued deteriorating well beyond the link-up time for extract. The Marines classified this as a Sea State 5–6. Although we were operating in the tropics, hypothermia was still possible in the 80-degree (27 Celcius) water due to the wind, rain, and possible exposure time. The plan indicated that we would be inserting at dusk, operating at night, and linking up for extract by 3:00 a.m.

My gear was a Marine Corps recon fighting load for amphibious operations, which included a weapon with 220 rounds of ammo, knife, compass, strobe, survival gear, one MRE, two 2-quart (2-L) canteens, water purification tabs, magnesium block, mask, fins, booties, pack with mission-essential gear, poncho, radio, night vision gear, and extra 550 cord. All of this was waterproofed in a swimmer's bundle to swim to the beach. A swimmer's bundle is a waterproof pack with the gear waterproofed inside. The pack is also dummy-corded to your wrist to ensure you don't lose it while swimming. Each of us was wearing an underwater dive team (UDT) vest, which included a carbon dioxide power inflator and a tube with a mouthpiece to blow air into the vest. This was our life vest in case we ran into any problems.

The insert left a lot to be desired. Because of the weather, we had to lower the zodiacs from the PHM in 6–12 feet (2–4m) seas. Trying to lower the craft, start the engines and get away from the PHM so the zodiacs would not get caught under its hull was a big challenge. Timing was everything and from the start things were difficult and bad. The insert was not going as planned and the zodiacs were not lowering nicely into the water, but instead went down sideways so that packs and paddles that were latched on the boat fell out. This meant a Marine or two had to jump into the sea to retrieve the gear. We *don't* lose gear in the Marine Corps. That hiccup added to an already stressful situation, but the Marines accomplish their missions, so we charged on. We got our boats inserted, rallied up at our insertion point and started to make our way to our target beach. We were about 1 ½ hours behind schedule when we departed the insertion point and the weather seemed to be getting worse.

Thankfully, the transit to the beachhead was somewhat uneventful. The swells were still large and we made it to our target beach banged up, but we were still behind schedule and did not make up any time.

We got our swimmers into the water 0.6 miles (1,000 m) out from the beach. We finned in, set-up security on the flanks and the hinterland, and put swimmers back in the water to check the bottom composition while other Marines hit the beach and gathered additional information for our mission. Our Confirmatory Beach Report went well once we hit the beach. We got all of the required line items for our report and headed back out to sea to link-up with our zodiacs. Again, we donned our fins, grabbed our weapons, swimmer's bundle, entered the surf-zone, and finned out. Link-up with our zodiacs went without a hitch. That was the end of our good fortune. We all know Murphy's law: Anything that can go wrong will go wrong. What I discovered that night is that if things do go wrong, the situation will quickly spiral downward. We Marines were ready to deal with contingencies. After all, that is how we have been trained, but ol' Murph had some tricks up his sleeves during the dark morning hours in bad sea conditions.

We started our transit to link up with the PHM, but the sea state was deteriorating: the waves and swells were getting bigger, a hard rain started to fall, and we began taking on water in all three of our zodiacs. The engine in the third boat began having problems that prevented it from keeping up. In turn, boats one and two had to slow down. The poor weather conditions put an additional strain on the engines, which in turn ate up the boats' limited fuel. To make matters worse, one of the fuel bladders in my boat had sprung a leak. So in addition to facing huge swells and taking on water, the leaking gas was seeping out on the aluminum deck and saturating our trousers, creating a new potential problem: chemical burns. Meanwhile, my boat and another zodiac started losing air in the gunnel tubes that hold down the boats' aluminum decking. Although we tried replacing the air with a foot pump, we couldn't keep pace with the leak and the boat became increasingly flimsy and soft, making it difficult to maneuver and easier to take on more water. This was not good at all for the eight Marines in the zodiac. Because one of the boats was leaking badly and the decking was coming undone, we decided to transfer the eight Marines in that boat to the two additional zodiacs and tow the damaged zodiac. We were overloaded and towing the crippled zodiac yet, continued to make our way to link-up for extract.

A thousand thoughts ran through my head as we slowly made our way to the PHM: *Are we going to make extract on time? Is the PHM going to be where it is supposed to be? Are we navigating correctly? Are the boats going to make it? Am I going to have to swim for it? If so, should I swim back to the beach?* We were all thinking the same thing: *Are we going to have to swim for it because our zodiacs are falling apart?* Although we all kept level heads and no one panicked, there was clearly concern and consternation etched on our faces. Some of the Marines joked about us all ending up as shark or fish bait. I remember joking about a supposed immediate action drill for when you see a shark: stab your buddy and swim away. Let the shark go after the blood and your buddy. We were all trying to add some levity to what was a stressful situation.

I also kept thinking about my training and the gear that I had with me—a pack that floated, my UDT vest that I could inflate as a last resort, my teammates, and the fact that I was a very strong swimmer and could swim just about anywhere. We kept driving on to our link-up point and we finally started to see lights out on the horizon. This surely had to be our PHM that we were approaching. The link up time was right, the location was right, and as we kept moving forward the lights got more visible and the outline of a large ship appeared.

In the meantime, both of the other zodiacs began leaking and the decking that held the boats up was beginning to buckle and come undone. Both boats were overloaded, but we kept trudging along to our link-up point. My calculations estimated by the time we made link-up we were about 7-8 miles (11–13km) out to sea. The sea state was still bad, and there was no way we would be able to pull our boats up onto the deck of the PHM. We did try a few times, but gravity, the weight of the zodiacs, the engines, and all of the gear made us soon realize it was not going to happen. Murphy struck again.

With three boats that were continuing to fall apart, being 7 miles (11km) out at sea, what were we going to do? We stayed in the boats we were in, kept the one zodiac in tow, and started to limp back to the coast. We moved along slowly back to the confines of the base and boathouse. A safety boat was put in the water that stayed with us all the way back to the base. We eventually made it, and arrived at dawn with calm seas, broken boats, and fatigued bodies and minds. We lost zero gear, accomplished our mission, no one was injured, but it was the most stressful time I've had in the water.

Lessons Learned

1. **Trust in my gear.** Even though the boats were deflating and taking on water, they still got us to our link-up point and back to the coast

2. **Trust in my teammates.** It is often said that misery loves company. We were all miserable, wanting to finish our mission, do preventative maintenance on our gear, get some warm chow in our bellies, and shower. As leaders, we rose to the occasion. Despite being in an awful situation that felt like it would never end, we all got through it together.

3. **Trust that things will go wrong.** Know that things are not going to always go as planned. When the first shots get fired, the plan goes out the window. It is time to improvise, rely on your contingency planning and training, and trust in your fellow teammates to get through a difficult situation. Be adaptable and flexible and know that if there is an opportunity for Mr. Murphy to show up and throw a wrench in your plan, he will. Deal with the situation by modifying your plan or objectives. Keep your head up, do what you can to persevere and you will make it through what life throws at you.

4. **Trust my mind and body.** If I said there were not any lows during the early morning hours I would be a liar. I was soaking wet, worried about all of us getting back safely, and I was literally sitting in gasoline for hours. I had a chemical burn that eventually healed and went away. This was a bad situation that did not last forever. I kept telling myself that I would get through it and I kept reassur-

ing my teammates we would get through this situation. The weather could not stay bad forever and we would have smooth, calm seas to make it home. Fortunately, we did and I can say we are stronger mentally for getting through the Amphibious Operation from Hell.

ABOUT JOEL STEVENS

Joel grew up in the Midwest where his father and grandfather always preached to him about self-reliance and being able to live off the land if things got bad. He graduated from the University of Northern Iowa with a Bachelor of Arts in Spanish and completed advanced computer work at George Washington University. Joel is a former United States Marine infantry officer and attended several military schools in the Quantico, Virginia, area. Joel had been thinking about TEOTWAWKI before Michael Stipe and R.E.M. penned the song "It's the End of the World as We Know It."

While at the University of Northern Iowa, Joel was a Division I swimmer and is still an avid participant in masters swimming, where he competes in sprint distance races. Joel is an enthusiastic outdoorsman and spends much of his free time in the mountains hunting, hiking, mountain biking, SCUBA diving, and sailing. Joel's hobby is researching survival gear and weapons as well as prepping for survival situations. Joel also has an interest in bug out vehicles that require no fossil fuels, as well as sailboats and mountain bikes. Joel operates several of the top survival blogs including SurvivalCache.com, SHTFBlog.com, and TheSurvivalistBlog.com. Joel also works at Forge Survival Supply, which sells survival gear and training to government agencies and the public.

Q&A WITH JOEL STEVENS

How long have you been thinking about and preparing for survival?
Growing up in southeast Iowa, I spent a lot of time in the woods gaining survival skills. I was also very active in the Boy Scouts and my parents often took me camping. With an active Army ammunition plant close by we spent our lives under a potential nuclear threat from the former Soviet Union. My father took that threat very seriously and was big into planning for worst-case scenarios. So I guess you could say I have been into survival since I was a little kid.

Please describe your everyday carry items.
I like to carry an HK P2000SK .40 caliber pistol with an extra magazine, a Spyderco Manix2 knife, Suunto Core watch, iPhone 4s with Mophie backup battery, Aurora Firestarter, and a Leatherman Charge ALX.3.

What is your favorite bug out pistol?
A Glock 17.

Favorite concealed carry pistol?
I have two: the HK P2000 SK .40 caliber and a Springfield Armory XD Sub-Compact .40 caliber with Trijicon night sights.

Joel Stevens

Favorite bug out rifle or carbine??

I use the Primary Weapon Systems' 18-inch (46cm) .223 Wylde designated marksman rifle.

What about shotguns? What do you prefer?

My Benelli M-4 desert camo combat shotgun.

How much bug-in food do you keep at your house? At your bug out location?

I keep two years' worth at each location.

Name the most important items in your bug out bag.

For me, the basics include: a Wiggy's sleeping bag with bivy, an MSR water purifier, Kel-tec Sub 2000 (9mm) rifle, AlpineAire meals, survival fishing kit, BlastMatch fire starter, and Gortex tops and bottoms. For a cold-weather environment I would be packing much more gear, including warming layers, a sleeping bag, possibly a tent, a stove, and cooking gear.

Describe your bug out location.

Let's just say it's in the Rocky Mountains.

Describe your bug out vehicle.

My vehicle of choice is a 1998 Ford Expedition or 2004 Honda Rincon ATV with a trailer. My mountain bike is going with me on both options.

What is your ideal bug out bag?

Granite Gear's Chief Patrol Pack in MultiCam.

Favorite home defense pistol?

An FNP-45 USG pistol with an M6 laser light. (It's hard to argue with 15 rounds of .45 automatic colt pistol for home defense.)

Favorite survival book?
The *SAS Handbook* by John "Lofty" Wiseman or *How to Survive the End of the World as We Know It* by James Wesley Rawles.

Favorite survival-type movie?
The Road Warrior

Favorite survival knife?
A Fallkniven A1.

Survival tools in your kit?
It's always good to have a Leatherman close by.

Have you ever found yourself in a survival situation? What happened, what were the circumstances, and what did you do to get out of it?
Everyone will face a moment in their life where their very survival is put on the line. It may be a quick decision to avoid a swerving truck or something much more severe like being stranded in the middle of the ocean. Although I have had many close calls with the Grim Reaper, there is one that sticks out in my mind as something that could have gone horribly wrong but luckily for me my training kicked in and I didn't panic.

It was late October of 2011. I was hunting elk in Medicine Bow-Routt National Forest outside of Craig, Colorado, with several friends who were visiting from out East. Routt National Forest is big country with over 2 million acres. It is a place where you can literally disappear. I was paired with my friend Korey. We hunted high and low on the mountains, but there were no elk to be found. Around 4:00 p.m. as the sun was setting in the late-autumn sky we decided to call it quits. We had hunted from 8,000 feet (2,438m) to 10,500 feet (3,200m) and crossed several mountains in search of the elk herd that never materialized. With the sun fading, Korey and I decided to head back to base camp to scout some areas for the next day's hunt.

Back at the camp, we dropped our heavy packs and grabbed some cold drinks while heading for the ATVs for our scouting trip. After getting skunked for a few days and seeing zero elk, Korey and I decided we would travel by ATV to another mountain area and scout for animal signs. After riding for 20 minutes deeper into the forest we found what appeared to be a service road or trail. Based on the snow still on the ground no humans had entered that trail for at least a few days. We drove our ATVs up the trail for about a mile (1.6km) until the path became too difficult to continue on ATV.

Korey and I then dismounted and proceeded to scout into the trees for animal signs. By this time the sun had set and we were quickly loosing daylight. We had one handheld GPS unit between us and marked the spot of our ATVs, thinking that the return would be no big deal. After traveling several hundred yards we came across elk tracks. Of course, we got excited and decided to follow them. Unfortunately, we then came across human footprints. This dampened our spirits quite a bit, but we decided to soldier on to see if we could find a good spot to set up the next day. At some point before it turned into total darkness we decided we'd better head back. Korey had a head lamp and led the way back to the ATVs following our foot prints.

After walking for about 20 minutes, I heard Korey say "I got a problem up here." I ran up to see what he was talking about. "I can't tell which foot prints are ours; they are going all different ways." At the time we thought we were still good, because we could not be more than a few hundred yards from the ATVs and eventually we would come across them.

As we stood there, I checked the GPS. The GPS arrow was flickering between north and west and wasn't giving us an exact way to travel. This happens sometimes when you are close to your objective and the GPS can access data from only a few satellites, as was the case in our location in the mountains.

That is when we made a stupid mistake. We decided to split up. At the time it seemed like a good idea. We thought we were relatively close to the ATVs and light was going away quickly so we wanted to find them, fast, before it got dark.

We were lightly equipped. Korey and I both had winter hunting clothes on with good boots and socks. We both were carrying flashlights, some light snacks, hunting rifles, and hunting knives. I also had a fire starter and a water purification straw. If Korey had any other gear, I was not aware of it. We both were planning for a short stay in the woods; our handheld radios were dropped in our heavy packs. Our cell phones were back in our trucks because there was no cell phone coverage in Routt.

This terrain was different than other terrain we had hunted in Routt. The area was heavily wooded with rolling hills but was not mountainous. It was somewhat of a valley with large mountains on either side. We made a quick plan. Korey would head off to his right and would swing back to the left, looking for the trail or me. I would do just the opposite. As we both headed off the terrain became more difficult. Dusk quickly turned into pitch black. The moon seemed to disappear and quickly I found myself not only lost in Routt National Forest but I was alone. I expected to be alone for 10 to 15 minutes and hopefully find the trail and wait for Korey or just find Korey.

After hiking for about 20 minutes I had neither found the trail nor Korey. I called Korey's name as loudly as I could. Nothing. That's when I thought, *Man, this was really stupid*. With the temperature quickly dropping into the 20s (7-10 Celsius) and being completely lost, the realization that I was going to have to spend the night out in the forest was quickly becoming a reality. I was also concerned about the other hunters back at base camp. What would they do? They had no idea where we went; they assumed we would be back long before dark.

I decided that rather than getting more lost, I would stay put for a bit and call Korey's name to see if he would come within earshot of my location. After about an hour it was clear to me that Korey was not coming toward me. I was going to have to strike out on my own or stay the night in the woods.

I had already done a quick inventory of what I had on me: a few snack bars, a bottle of water, fire starter, compass, GPS, map, water purification straw, extra ammo, hat, gloves, a pullover jacket, and a hunting rifle. Not exactly ideal camping gear for the Rocky Mountains. After staying put for quite some time I decided to strike out in one general direction using my compass and keeping a pace count. I also marked my location on the GPS, on the ground, and on the map. My idea was to walk in one general direction for 400 yards (366m), call for Korey and then walk back if I did not find him. Hopefully along those 400 yards (366m), I would run into either the ATVs or the trail. If I found nothing, I would turn around and walk the azimuth back to where I started, or close to it, then start off on a new direction. I marked my starting position on the ground by piling up a group of sticks in a way that I would know was mine. I basically was creating my own search area rather than just walking aimlessly in the mountains.

The woods were quiet, dark, and cold. I set out on my first 400-pace march. I tried to stay on the same course the whole time but the terrain was difficult and I spent more time tripping and falling rather than looking at my compass. After I reached my 400-pace limit, I called out to Korey. Nothing. I stood there for another 15 minutes calling out again and again. Still nothing. Discouraged, I turned around and starting walking the 400 paces back to my starting point. Somehow I found my pile of sticks that I started from, which still surprises me to this day. I stopped again to call for Korey. Nothing.

By this time I was getting pretty cold. Korey and I had dropped our heavy jackets for light, pullover sweatshirts. My extremities were good. I had a good winter hat and gloves on and my feet felt fine thanks to a solid pair of hunting boots with good wool socks. However, my core was starting to get cold. All of the walking had generated sweat and being lightly-clothed was making me cold fast.

I decided that I needed to complete my search of the area before camping for the night. I was already dreading the camping sequence but I knew I could do it. I would get a fire going then collect enough wood to last me for the night. Then I would create some type of bedding to sit on. I wasn't planning on laying down because I knew that I would get too cold. There was also not enough snow to consider things like a snow cave so I was stuck with sitting on the cold ground. After the mental exercise of camping was out of my head, I took the azimuth that I had just completed and added 90 degrees to it.

Again, I started trekking out my 400 paces, calling for Korey here and there. At about 250 paces I came across what appeared to be a clearing in the woods. I took my flashlight and shined it around. I had stumbled across the trail, or at least a trail. I quickly walked down the trail and located the ATVs. I immediately noticed Korey's ATV was still there and had not been touched. He was still lost. The time was quickly closing in on 10:00 p.m. and I knew the other hunters would be worried about us.

I figured that the sound of the ATV engine would be the best bet for Korey to find his way out of the woods. So I fired up my ATV and gave it the gas. I also began cruising up and down the trail back to the main road. The whole time I was cranking the engine to make as much noise as possible. After about five passes I saw Korey on the trail. He looked a little worried but no major damage. We exchanged stories and relief. He had decided that he was lost and would just sit out the night until daylight. He said if it hadn't been for the noise of the ATV he would have stayed in the woods all night.

This is just a quick story about how something so innocent can turn tragic in a minute. Luckily for Korey and me we were woodsmen and knew the basics of survival, and had some gear with us. Although we were scared and worried, we never panicked. The weather gods were nice to us that night and we did not have to deal with rain or snow. And although it was very cold outside that night, there was almost no wind to speak of, which is almost unheard of in the mountains. It was a long ride back to base camp on the ATVs. The other guys were indeed worried about us and were just about to sound the alarm.

That event has scarred me forever. I now make sure I have essential gear with me at all times and I think about the little things like: 1) Who knows where I am; 2) Who knows where I am going; 3) Who knows what time I will be back.

Korey and I made a lot of mistakes that day. Being at 10,000 feet (3,048m) in sub-freezing temperatures with no 9-1-1 to call could have cost us our lives. Luckily, it didn't.

GEAR APPENDIX

PACK

Granite Gear, Inc.
2312 10th Street
Two Harbors, MN 55616
218-834-6157
granitegear.com

SealLine
Cascade Designs
4000 First Avenue South
Seattle, WA 98134
206-505-9500
cascadedesigns.com/sealline

HIPBAG

Maxpedition
P.O. Box 5008
Palos Verdes, CA 90274
310-768-0098
maxpedition.com

HEADLAMP

Petzl
2929 Decker Lake Drive
Salt Lake City, UT 84119
801-926-1500
petzl.com

COMPASS

Suunto
Valimotie 7
FI-01510
Vantaa Finland
855-258-0900
suunto.com/compass-collections

BIVY SACK AND FIRST AID KITS

Adventure Medical Kits
7700 Edgewater Drive
Suite 526
Oakland, CA 94621
800-324-3517
adventuremedicalkits.com

SLEEPING BAG

Wiggy's, Inc.
P.O. Box 2124
Grand Junction, CO 81502
866-411-6465
wiggys.com

PONCHOS

Liberty Mountain
9816 South Jordan Gateway
(500 W)
Sandy, UT 84070
800-366-2666
libertymountain.com

Equinox
1307 Park Avenue
Williamsport, PA 17701
877-322-5909
equinoxltd.com

FIRE STARTERS

Aurora Fire Starter
Solo Scientific
P.O. Box 565
New Hartford, NY 13413
888-248-8233
soloscientific.com

BlastMatch Fire Starter and WetFire Tinder
Ultimate Survival
Technologies
7720 Philips Highway
Jacksonville, FL 32256
877-738-3738
ultimatesurvival.com

Stormproof Matches
Industrial Revolution, Inc.
5835 Segale Park Drive C
Tukwila, WA 98188
888-297-6062
industrialrev.com/uco

EMERGENCY WATER AND FOOD

Mainstay Food and Water Rations
Survivor Industries, Inc.
1621 Emerson Avenue
Oxnard, CA 93033
805-385-5560
survivorind.com

STOVES AND COOKING GEAR

Mountain Safety Research
4000 First Avenue, South
Seattle, WA 98134
206-505-9500
cascadedesigns.com/msr

WATER FILTRATION

Mountain Safety Research
4000 First Avenue, South
Seattle, WA 98134
206-505-9500
cascadedesigns.com/msr

Aquamira Technologies, Inc.
917 West 600 North
Logan, UT 84321
877-644-4650
aquamira.com

KNIVES

Gerber Gear
14200 SW 72nd Avenue
Portland, OR 97224
800-950-6161
gerbergear.com

Parry Blade
WBC & Associates
Oxted
Surrey
RH8 9JD
United Kingdom
+44 (0)1883 714456
parryblade.com

FallKniven
Fällkniven AB
Granatvägen 8
96143 Boden
Sweden
+4692154422
fallkniven.com

MULTITOOL

Leatherman
Leatherman Tool Group, Inc.
P.O. Box 20595
Portland, OR 97294
800-847-8665
leatherman.com

FISHING GEAR

Bestglide
Best Glide ASE, Inc.
105 East Ward
Robinson, TX 76706
888-834-9971
bestglide.com

SURVIVAL RADIO

Midland Survival Radios
ExploraTrack
P.O. Box 1190
Cannon Beach, OR 97110
800-414-8655
midlandweatherradios.com

In addition to the individual websites, you can find all of this gear at
forgesurvivalsupply.com

INDEX

Dedication

We would like to thank our families who put up with endless hours of work on this book. Our parents, who showed us the right way to live. Our team of dedicated survivalists at SurvivalCache.com and SHTFBlog.com who encouraged us with this book. Our brothers and sisters in arms, especially those wearing the Eagle, Globe, and Anchor—stay motivated, prepared, and ever vigilant against our nation's foes.

About the Authors

Mark Puhaly graduated from Texas A&M University with a BS in biochemistry and completed graduate work in international commerce and policy at George Mason University. Mark is a former Marine recon team leader, Marine officer instructor at The Basic School and Marine infantry officer. He is an avid outdoor adventurist and survivalist. Mark has lived and traveled all over the world with the Marine Corps and as a civilian. He has raced multiple marathons and triathlons. He is currently training for his next Ironman triathlon and coaches triathletes, swimmers and crossfit athletes. When Mark is not working or coaching he is preparing for his next endurance race or spending time with his family.

Joel Stevens had been thinking about TEOTWAWKI long before R.E.M. penned the song *It's The End of the World as We Know It*. Joel grew up in the Midwest where his father and grandfather always preached to him about self-reliance and being able to live off the land. Joel stayed in the Midwest for college where he was a Division I swimmer and school record holder. After college, Joel joined the Marine Corps where he served as a Marine Infantry Officer. Joel is an avid outdoorsman and spends much of his free time in the mountains hunting, hiking, and mountain biking or near the ocean scuba diving and sailing. Joel's hobby is researching survival gear and weapons as well as prepping for survival situations. Joel also has an interest in bug out vehicles that don't require fossil fuels, such as sailboats and mountain bikes.

Other fine Living Ready books are available from your local bookstore and online suppliers. Visit our website, www.livingreadyonline.com. Living Ready® is a registered trademark of F+W Media.

18 17 16 15 14   5 4 3 2 1

ISBN-13: 978-1-4403-3843-4

Distributed in Canada by Fraser Direct
100 Armstrong Avenue, Georgetown, Ontario, Canada L7G 5S4, Tel: (905) 877-4411

Distributed in the U.K. and Europe by F&W Media International, LTD
Brunel House, Forde Close, Newton Abbot, TQ12 4PU, UK, Tel: (+44) 1626 323200,
Fax: (+44) 1626 323319, E-mail: enquiries@fwmedia.com

Distributed in Australia by Capricorn Link
P.O. Box 704, S. Windsor NSW, 2756 Australia, Tel: (02) 4560-1600, Fax: (02) 4577-5288,
E-mail: books@capricornlink.com.au

Edited by Kelly Messerly and Kelsea Daulton
Designed by Clare Finney
Production coordinated by Debbie Thomas
Photos by Nathan Rigaud unless otherwise noted

FREE SURVIVAL KIT PACKING LISTS

Download printable versions of the survival kit packing lists found in this book for free at www.livingreadyonline.com/urbanemergency. The download includes packing lists for:

- Everyday Carry Items
- Workplace Emergency Kits
- Get-Home Bag
- Vehicle Emergency Kit
- Bug-Out Bag

MORE BOOKS ON SURVIVAL AND PREPAREDNESS

Build The Perfect Bug Out Vehicle by Creek Stewart

Living Ready Pocket Manual: First Aid by James Hubbard, The Survival Doctor™

Food Storage For Self-Sufficiency and Survival by Angela Paskett

AVAILABLE ONLINE AND IN BOOKSTORES EVERYWHERE!

Join our mailing list at www.livingreadyonline.com.

Become a fan of our Facebook page: facebook.com/LivingReady